"Michael Novak changed history in 1982 with the publication of *The Spirit of Democratic Capitalism*. In a clarifying instant we were enabled to see, as he now writes, that "the business corporation has been the voluntary association through which Americans have wrought the economic revolution that changed the world's horizons." Ours no less. We could now see the moral dimension of the corporation—the potential for moral and also immoral conduct. We could now identify the singularity of the American experience. But that was fifteen years ago! Vast changes have since occurred. And here again is our preeminent moral philosopher pursuing events, finding meaning. A profound experience awaits the reader."

—*Senator Daniel Patrick Moynihan*, D-NY

"Those concerned for the world's poor recognize the crippling dependency created by yesterday's aid programs. Today, from Bogota to Bangladesh, the "least among us" are transforming their lives—not through hand-outs, but through small loans they use to launch microenterprises. Michael Novak aptly describes what both large Western corporations and tiny third world microenterprises know instinctively: the right of voluntary association liberates the human spirit to create wealth, escape poverty, and meet human needs."

—*Jim Damron*
Director of Marketing
Opportunity International

"Michael Novak has applied his incomparable philosophical insight to the principles of business from which businesses can draw ever more practical guidance."

—*Robert W. Galvin*
Chairman of the Executive Committee
Motorola Inc.

"Michael Novak has provided a cogent and very timely exposition on the future of the corporation, intellectual property rights and corporate governance. In this book it is abundantly clear that the development of the public corporation was a direct outgrowth of a direct contribution to the principles of constitutional law, the benefit of meritocracy and the enhancement of civil society. This book is a message not only to the concerned citizen, but is particularly important to business leaders "to be philosophically vigilant—that is principled and unrelenting against the trespasses of government power on private property." This book also makes clear the benefits of increased productivity and scientific and technological progress obtained under a system of "protected patents and copyrights." This system has resulted in "an explosion in invention and discovery far beyond anything achieved under non-patent regimes." This book, therefore, is a must for every student of freedom, every public policy maker concerned with economic progress, and every business person concerned with the interests of consumers and shareholders alike."

—*John M. Templeton, M.D.*
President
John Templeton Foundation

"With thoughtfulness and verve, Michael Novak demonstrates once again why he is the most respected authority on American business and culture. In *The Fire of Invention* he identifies something many scholars continue to ignore: the precious link between individual liberty, the entrepreneurial spirit, and capitalism. Novak's trenchant observations, well-grounded and well-argued, draw upon his vast knowledge of American history and corporate America, and will be an education for business and political leaders alike."

—*William E. Simon*
President
John M. Olin Foundation, Inc.

"In *The Fire of Invention*, Michael Novak reminds us that the business corporation is not merely a necessary evil to be tolerated, but an integral part of our democratic order critical to both civic and public life. He forthrightly rejects trendy attempts to recycle socialist ideas from the "stakeholder society" to strictures against downsizing, while pointing us to the true sources of creativity in the postindustrial world."

—*Francis Fukuyama*
Omer L. and Nancy Hirst Professor of Public Policy

"I have read a lot of business writers, but Novak is special—straight and true, not going with the fads. This book is essential reading for practitioners of business."

—*James Vincent*
Chairman/CEO
Biogen

"In this book, Michael Novak reemphasizes the fact that the publicly owned corporation, albeit with some internal flaws, has proven to be the most effective instrument for creating the products and services by which the members of society can improve their lives. The author explores the key role played by patent and copyright laws in this process, as well as their philosophical foundation. Michael Novak forewarns about the choppy waters into which corporations are starting to sail and about the rocks lurking below the water surface. As an example, he points out how words such as "corporate governance," "corporate responsibility" and "environmentalism," among others, are being used in place of, or as a disguise for old-line socialist ideas such as the need for directed economic planning or the requirement that corporations' primary purpose be to benefit all stakeholders. In a sense, this book is a call to business executives to stand up in defense of the independence of the most powerful economic machine known to man—the publicly owned corporation. Or, otherwise, to paraphrase a line from a popular country song, if one doesn't stand for something, one will fall for anything. A must-read book for every CEO."

—*Roberto C. Goizueta*
CEO
The Coca Cola Company

"The shape of business in the 21st century is being formed right now. And no one is more in the center of the discussion than Michael Novak. This book must be read by anyone serious about the future of America. Its ideas will change the lives of millions."

—Robert L. Dilenschneider
The Dilenschneider Group, Inc.

"In *The Fire of Invention* Michael Novak does what we have come to expect of him: write on matters of capitalism and corporate governance in an eloquent, illuminating and morally serious manner. He understands as few others do the great promise, as well as the limits and temptations, of democratic capitalism."

—William J. Bennett
Author of *The Book of Virtues*

"In *The Fire of Invention*, Michael Novak, analyst of the conscience of corporate America, points out the overwhelming significance of the corporation, not only for business, but for civil society as a whole. He places appropriate emphasis on the protection of intellectual property rights for providing incentives for investment, generating wealth, and providing employment. He warns against government mandates and other pressures for unwise reforms, especially regarding corporate governance, that would stifle initiative and creativity; and he denounces corporate appeasement. Why undermine the very attributes that have been responsible for the most successful society the world has ever known? Intellectual leaders—and in particular, businessmen—should recognize the importance of the corporation, be sensitive to its fragility, and be alarmed by subtle efforts to undermine its unique strengths."

—*Robert H. Malott*
Chairman, Executive Committee
FMC Corporation

"In an era of glib political correctness, where defeated socialists have turned their fire on the corporation, Michael Novak takes us back to basics to inquire what is a corporation, what is its purpose, and how best that purpose can be advanced. His analysis and insight should become the framework for preserving the enterprise association."

—*Walter B. Wriston*
Citicorp

"Michael Novak articulates the great human good coming from business and free markets. He urges corporations to represent "shareholders" rather than "stakeholders." Corporate leaders should use this book as a defense manual against those who would shift to them the unwisely assumed responsibilities of the state."

—*Joseph J. Jacobs, Ph. D.*
Jacobs Engineering Group, Inc.

"Novak throws light on the most resilient and creative, but least appreciated institution of modern times: the business corporation. His discussion of the relation between the business corporation, civil society, and the (political) state is especially clear and useful."

—*Russell Hittinger*
Warren Professor of Catholic Studies
The University of Tulsa

"Michael Novak is our country's soundest thinker and foremost authority on the ethical foundations of the free market economy. This volume, another of Mr. Novak's gems, develops and extends his insights into the moral and practical benefits of capitalism."

—*Drayton Nabers*
Chairman and CEO
Protective Life Corporation

"Capitalism has won the war against socialism, this we all know; however, as Michael Novak warns us, a battle still rages to socialize the American corporation. This book serves as a wake-up call to Corporate America to stand up to this challenge rather than capitulate through appeasement."

—*J. B. Fuqua*
Chairman of the Board
Fuqua Enterprises, Inc.

"With his usual intellectual vigor, Michael Novak extends his philosophical and social interpretation of the modern corporation, defending its innovative creativity against challenges old and new. He is sure to delight every advocate of the chief organizational instrument of today's global economy, and sure to enrage every lingering socialist."

—*Max Stackhouse*
Princeton Theological Seminary

THE FIRE
·OF·
INVENTION

Selected Books by Michael Novak

Ascent of the Mountain, Flight of the Dove

•

Belief and Unbelief

•

The Spirit of Democratic Capitalism

•

Business as a Calling: Work and the Examined Life

•

*Freedom with Justice: Catholic Social Thought
and Liberal Institutions*

•

Free Persons and the Common Good

•

The Catholic Ethic and the Spirit of Capitalism

•

Choosing Presidents

•

The Experience of Nothingness

•

The Guns of Lattimer

•

The Joy of Sports

•

The New Consensus on Family and Welfare (EDITOR)

•

The Open Church

•

*Taking Glasnost Seriously: Toward an
Open Soviet Union*

•

*This Hemisphere of Liberty: A Philosophy
of the Americas*

•

To Empower People: From State to Civil Society (EDITOR)

•

Toward a Theology of the Corporation

•

Unmeltable Ethnics

•

Will It Liberate: Questions about Liberation Theology

THE FIRE
·OF·
INVENTION

Civil Society and the
Future of the Corporation

MICHAEL NOVAK

ROWMAN & LITTLEFIELD PUBLISHERS, INC.
Lanham • Boulder • New York •Oxford

ROWMAN & LITTLEFIELD PUBLISHERS, INC.

Published in the United States of America
by Rowman & Littlefield Publishers, Inc.
4720 Boston Way, Lanham, Maryland 20706

12 Hid's Copse Road
Cummor Hill, Oxford OX2 9JJ, England

British Library Cataloging in Publication Information
Available

Library of Congress Cataloging-in-Publication Data

Novak, Michael.
    The fire of invention : civil society and the future of the
corporation / Michael Novak.
        p.   cm.
    Includes bibliographical references and index.
    ISBN 0-8476-8664-7 (cloth : alk. paper)
    1. Corporations—Forecasting.
HD2731.N679   1997
338.7′01′12—dc21   97-18755
                                                        CIP

ISBN 0-8476-8664-7 (cloth : alk. paper)

Printed in the United States of America

♾™ The paper used in this publication meets the
minimum requirements of American National Standard
for Information Sciences—Permanence of Paper for
Printed Library Materials, ANSI Z39.48–1984.

for

MICHAEL A. SCULLY

•

Friend
Perceptive Writer
Far-seeing Editor
Wise Business Executive

•

1949–1996
Rest in Peace

"The Corporation,
as we know it—and we know it
from every aspect
of our lives—was invented;
it did not come to be
of itself."

•

OSCAR HANDLIN

CONTENTS

ACKNOWLEDGMENTS

My thanks go to my research associate, Brian Anderson, who worked himself into a bout in the hospital over this project (as well as over his own splendid manuscript on Raymond Aron), and whose outstanding work, although present on every page, is most visible in the footnotes.

Thanks, too, to Cathie Love, our cheerful (well, usually cheerful) secretary, who mostly refrains from complaining about versions and drafts that exceed ten—or even twenty—retypings!

In addition, I am grateful to the Pfizer Corporation, and in particular to Terence Gallagher and Carson Daly, for sponsoring the Pfizer Lectures at the American Enterprise Institute, for inviting me to turn my mind to the problems faced by the business corporation fifteen years after I had written *Toward a Theology of the Corporation*—and for not taking no for an answer.

I have dedicated this volume to my longtime friend Michael A. Scully, the first editor of *This World*, a journal we jointly founded in 1982, and later director of Pfizer's Policy Communications Division. Better, lovelier, more civilized men are not often found. Michael Scully died, suddenly, at the age of 47, within weeks after we had last seen him at the third of these lectures. He represented, to my mind, the highest moral possibilities of corporate life.

I am very sorry Michael's young daughter, Grace Mary (three months old when he died), will not get to know him as she grows up—she deserves to know the high regard in which his friends and associates held him. Her father was a very good man, and many loved him well.

· *Introduction* ·

A Spirit Born from the Sea

To understand America's greatness, you have to understand the sea. America was born from the sea. From three sides, the sea surrounds America, and all the human beings who have struggled to thrive on these shores came from across the seas.

The first settlers, lost in the mists of distant history, came from Asia. When the first Europeans arrived, not more than eight million humans lived in the vast and empty territories now marked as the United States, mostly as wandering tribes; perhaps another million lived in Canada.

How, then, do we explain the eminence of American civilization so few generations later?

By the year 1776, when the United States declared its independence, its citizens numbered under 4 million against England's 40 million. For most basics of life they depended on their own enterprise, invention, and ingenuity. Then and for decades afterward most of their manufactured goods, and much else, came across the seas from England. For their sustenance, out of necessity, Americans took to the sea as though it were their native terrain.

"Today," Tocqueville wrote of the year 1832, "it is the Americans who carry to their shores nine-tenths of the products of Europe. It is the Americans too who carry three quarters of the exports of the New World to European consumers." He added, "They are born to rule the seas, as the Romans were to conquer the world."[1]

From the earliest period, the U.S. Navy was dauntless in defending the integrity of American private vessels at sea. Thomas Jefferson himself did not hesitate to make war on the Barbary pirates in the far-off Mediterranean. "Already the Americans can enforce respect for their flag," Tocqueville wrote a generation later; "soon they will be able to make it feared."

While the U.S. Navy protected the flag as needed, American seafaring was mostly a private undertaking of joint stock companies and individual merchants. The forest of masts in the American fleet was put to sea by private hands and manned by private captains and private seamen. "American ships fill the docks of Le Havre and Liverpool," Tocqueville wrote, "while the number of English vessels in New York harbor is comparatively small."

The sea gave Americans the space to be different from the rest of the world. (For a far longer time, Canada, Mexico, and all of Latin America declined to cut their umbilical cords to European political ideas.) Above all, it was the sea that set the pattern for American business, the business corporation and, at a more substantial level, the American character.

The sea made the Americans venturous. The sea taught Americans to love risk and to find zest in difficult things. The sea taught Americans a love for invention. The sea made Americans brave. And, of course, it was the sea that allowed Americans to be free. It permitted them to carry out their national experiment in freedom from the interference of foreign powers, foreign customs, foreign regulations, or, indeed, foreign fears and inhibitions.

Furthermore, Tocqueville noted, Americans exhibited at sea special intellectual and moral qualities. They were not aristocrats, accustomed to ease. They were sailing for themselves and to make a good future for their families. Their aim was not military, but economic. That aim led them to adopt new methods and to exhibit unprecedented superiorities that were—Tocqueville's words again—"purely intellectual and moral."

The European navigator is prudent about venturing out to sea, Tocqueville added. He waits for agreeable weather, furls some of his sails at night, seeks port often, and, paying for harborage the while, awaits favorable winds. The American sailor, by contrast, sets sail from Boston to China through fair weather and foul, keeps all sails to wind by night as well as day, repairs storm damage as he goes, avoids ports, is content with brackish water and salted meats, pauses in Canton no more than a few days, and having seen land only once, returns to Boston in under two years, and there sells his tea "a farthing cheaper than an English merchant can."

It is not calculation alone that leads the American, however; he is "obeying an impulse of his nature." What the French under Napoleon put into war, perplexing rival generals and toppling the most ancient monarchies of Europe, the Americans put into commerce. "I cannot express my thoughts better than by saying that the Americans put something heroic into their way of trading. It will always be very difficult for a European merchant to imitate his American competitor in this."

Tocqueville is a master at grasping the larger implications of each shrewdly observed fact. He sees that an American has all the wants and desires learned from the high civilization of Europe, yet has to provide for himself the various things that education and habit have made necessary for him, so that "one and the same man will till his fields, build his house, make his tools, cobble his shoes, and with his own hands weave the coarse cloth that covers him. This is bad for improving craftsmanship but greatly serves to develop the worker's intelligence."

A first consequence is that Americans easily change their trade, suiting their occupations to the needs of the moment. "One comes across those who have been in turn lawyers, farmers, merchants, ministers of the Gospel, and doctors." A second consequence is that, though the Americans may be less skillful in any of these crafts than a European specialist, their capacities are more general and the sphere of their intelligence is wider. A third is that the Americans are not held back by the axioms of craftsmen, the prejudices of professionals, the methods inherited from the past, or the habits of older civilizations. They know that their country is like no other and that their situation is unprecedented.

"The American," Tocqueville astutely observes, putting himself by a rare act of sympathy in American shoes, "lives in a land of wonders." The American is accustomed to frequent reversals of fortune, often witnessing the rich become poor and the poor become rich, old and famous families decline and even pass away, and new families never before heard of become famous and prosperous. For Americans, nothing is fixed, everything around them is in movement, and nearly always the new is synonymous with the improved.

This fact of American life, Tocqueville comments, leads to alertness and a general disposition to try harder to rise above the common level of humanity. For the Americans, "something which does not yet exist is just something that has not yet been tried." Americans love the new and the risky. "For an American the whole of life is treated like a game of chance, a time of revolution, or the day of battle."

In a land where individuals do everything for themselves and learn how to do many different things, and when they see all around them the benefits of ingenuity and *newness*, an irresistible impulse is given to the national character: "Choose any American at random, and he should be a man of burning desires, enterprising, adventurous, and, above all, an innovator." The American carries this bent with him into the backwoods, into the business of the cities, and out upon the seven seas. The New World has given birth to a new type of human being, whose most fascinating quality is his enchantment with the new—and his disdain for what Europe treasures: the prudent, the traditional, the tried, the solid, the fixed.

I have often thought, in visiting Europe some seven generations after the publication of Tocqueville's book, that this is why European innkeepers get red in the neck and *angry* when I do not accept their confident response, "We don't do that here." Instead, I insist on asking—in my sweetest voice—"But why not? Why couldn't you just . . . ?" and go on to explain how it *could* be done. European innkeepers do not like that and, most often, they will not accept advice. We turn away, they and I, in mutual frustration and mutual incomprehension. I imagine the innkeeper later telling associates about the impertinence of the Americans, their lack of respect for the way things are.

There is abroad in Europe still today—in Germany and France, especially—a profound contentment with the way things are and the rightness of custom. Many Europeans cling with vigor to the traditional allocation of responsibilities for thinking and acting, and to every inherited privilege, however modest, that gives one of them the final say on this or that, no questions asked. Even in the smallest details of life, Europeans seem always to be *protecting* an accepted order. I confess that in some ways this arrangement often seems restful, quaint, and even civilized. Life in Europe is often unusually pleasant. And yet, when working in Europe, I daily find myself at some point chafing; it is certain that I could not bear to live under such pleasantness for long. For such pleasure is best enjoyed when one does not wish to *do* anything or get anything *done*.

Obviously, Europeans continue to do much and even to innovate, but the amount of energy they must expend in learning hidden rules and patiently pushing things along accepted lines is staggeringly great. In addition to paying the high taxes and meeting the burdensome regulations of the State—all designed to protect a fantastic array of privileges and protected habits, eked out over centuries as entitlements—they must pay the enormous taxation of customs, manners, and methods. Americans learn their patriotic lessons in foreign postal zones.

Anthony de Jasay describes the French model of society in the years following the fall of socialism:

> America basically accepts capitalism, not least because it considers it quintessentially American. It is not the

principle that it questions, only the practice. France basically rejects capitalism, especially in principle, the more so as it considers it quintessentially "Anglo-Saxon."

De Jasay then goes on to describe how the French solve the problem of the collapse of socialism. Socialism has failed; he loathes capitalism—so what's a Frenchman to do? The French don't mind ownership, or even privilege; they cling to inheritances of both kinds passionately.

> In sharp contrast to personal patrimony—the house, the savings account, the share in uncle's farm and aunt's corner shop or sidewalk cafe, which both Left and Right hold sacrosanct—capital is despised on all sides. It is tolerated, however, because more than anywhere else, capital in France is repentant, tame, subservient to the bureaucracy of the state, conciliatory toward labor. A higher profile would not fit what the French like to regard as their specific system, a model of society no one else possesses, or at least not to the same extent. The model has three principal features: it is technocratic, medieval, and authoritarian.[2]

So it is that Europeans, even at the humblest levels of society, imitate the manners and methods of aristocrats: They all seem to think of themselves as having titles, at least in the sense of having wrested from the laws of the past certain entitlements and immunities. Even farmers and truck drivers, as was proved in

France in recent years, manifest a stunning righteousness in shutting down the rest of society to protect
their humble entitlements, a righteousness that seems
to Americans purely irrational and yet, astonishingly,
wins broad popular support in Europe.[3]

European workers do not argue that their occupa-
tional entitlements secure benefits for the common
good or have demonstrable practical benefits for others. They do not demand a reasoned public analysis
of costs and benefits. "No, an entitlement is an entitlement, let no one take it away, and that is the end of
the matter. Let the world stop. Let ruin come. We
shall not yield." Other Europeans halt in admiration,
nodding agreement. This is a belief in the good of
order, fixed order, outside the experience of any
American.

Many analysts go awry, I think, in arguing that
under the capitalism of the Rhine, the collective is preeminent, whereas under Anglo-American capitalism
there prevails the jungle of the anarchic individual.[4]
On the contrary, in America the *argument* nearly always centers on the general welfare, and when a majority can be persuaded that a special interest is hurt-
ing too many others, its entitlements are almost
certain to be renegotiated.

In Europe, the argument that many (or even all)
will benefit by a new arrangement does not still a
keenly felt duty to cling to past entitlements *because
they are entitlements from the past*. Everyone seems
afraid that once *that* dike is penetrated, they will lose

the sense of fixity and security that has come to seem as dear to them as the meaning of life itself.[5] In America, by contrast, the new has regularly been experienced as an improvement for all, or almost all. Thus, the argument that all will benefit, even if unequally, is socially potent.

In fact, it seems that under Rhenish capitalism, paradoxically, individual interests constantly prevail against public need. Under the American combination of democracy and capitalism, by contrast, a new deal for the whole society often wins consent from large majorities. Americans have learned to trust a malleable common order, because malleability has so often led to the improvement of their personal conditions. In this sense, the American political economy is more devoted to the common good than Europeans find it easy to imagine.

Thus, Europeans tend to explain away differences between European and American economic performance by caricaturing American life in denigrating ways. When they hear that the U.S. economy has created new jobs consistently from 1976 to 1996, year after year, under such diverse presidents as Carter, Reagan, Bush, and Clinton—50 million new jobs— while Europe lost jobs and watched unemployment levels climb into double digits, some Europeans sneer that they don't want 50 million new hamburger flippers. Europeans, they sniff, cherish high-paying jobs (as if Americans don't). They do not care to know that most of the new jobs in the United States pay higher than average salaries, and that many of them are in high-tech fields of communications and medicine that did not exist in 1986, let alone 1976.[6]

Between 1981 and 1990 alone, the value of the American personal computer industry grew from virtually nothing to $100 billion. This is, according to *The Economist*, "the largest legal increase of wealth in history."[7] This industry is now as large as, or larger than, the American automobile industry. Add to this the communications and aerospace industries, fiber optics, the Internet, and the transformation of mechanical processes to electronic processes. High-paying jobs, indeed!

Europeans pay a formidable price for their beloved security and stasis. They prefer the comfort of where they are to a better—but less certain—future. I do not begrudge them this. Had I experienced the European turmoil of the last ninety years, I might equally long for the world to stand in place for a generation or two. All I plead is that Europeans cease denigrating America because its experience has not been Europe's—that they try to open their eyes to a different reality; that they do not try to force America into the circle of their own understanding of history. Let them, for a beginning, take Tocqueville as a guide.

By contrast with Europe, as Tocqueville writes, America is afire with invention. Americans love risk.

Well, most Americans. Some Americans of the Left

(not all) would love to live in a social democracy of the Western European type. They imagine that European social democracies are "ahead" of the United States. They think this way because of European thinkers, whose modes of analysis they try in vain to import into America. They think their route to power is to make a large majority of Americans come to love security as much as Europeans love it, so as to become dependent on the State for supplying it, or rather, pretending to supply it. They preach, as though it were a good, the road to serfdom. There is fraud in what they offer.

Personal security for humans cannot be bought—or, more exactly, paid for. The American systems of support for those over age sixty-five—Social Security and Medicare—are each in its way gigantic pyramid schemes, distributed to others nearly as fast as they come in rather than being based upon investments in trust funds growing with "the magic of compound interest" for future withdrawal. The base of the pyramid, the rising tide of new workers already born, is far too small to bear the immense overhanging burden, particularly since the average age of death of current recipients keeps climbing ever higher—above sixty-five, above seventy, above eighty.[8] So the false dream of security is splintering against actuarial reality.

Another way to put this is that one set of "progressive" programs—especially abortion—have cut through the expected cohorts of the young like a scythe, dooming the other set of "progressive" programs, concerning universal security for the elderly. Abortion alone cut down 35 million Americans from the labor force between 1973 and 1995; these youngsters are no longer alive to support the elderly. Except for the millions of immigrants drawn to America, America's birth rates would be closer to the demographic tragedy now striking Europe—an ever steeper plunge in the number of women of child-bearing age, a "culture of death."[9]

The good news is that most Americans do not wish America to become like Europe. To security, most Americans prefer opportunity. Asked to choose between the importance of "equality of income or the freedom to live and develop without hindrance," Americans choose the latter by 71 percent, Europeans by 59 percent. And when asked which is more important—equality or freedom—Americans hold freedom to be more important by a margin of 72 percent to 20 percent. Italians, Germans, and Spaniards all weigh equality more heavily than freedom. Ask Europeans if they would prefer a world in which every part of the population would be better off, but in which there would be more rapid movement up and down the income ladder for individuals, and also greater inequalities. Most would probably say no. Americans prefer to take their chances.[10] That has been America's actual situation since its beginning.

Some 99 percent of Americans came to these shores poor. Today, even the poorest have seen their living standards advance to levels their grandparents would have found unimaginable, and by now all but 14 percent are above the poverty line (which the government sets at about $15,700 cash income per year per family of four). Thus, the American preference for mobility and fluidity is well-grounded in national and personal experience.

For virtually all Americans, coming to America has brought good fortune. Even for American blacks, who have suffered much injustice and faced unequalled obstacles, America has brought success that neither Africa nor any other place ever has. The combined income of America's 32 million blacks alone is larger than the GDP of all but ten nations of the world, and nearly as large as that of all of Africa's 800 million people combined—$300 billion v. $389 billion.[11]

For Americans, the new is a friend. For Americans, it is natural to think that the cause of the wealth of nations is inventiveness. American laws, American traditions, American customs, American habits—all are geared toward innovation. The world Americans live in is awash with new products and new services, new machinery, new devices. Every year's automobiles bring new wonders of technology, small changes, usually, but of increasing convenience and power. More and more, the dumb stuff of matter is being bent to instantaneous human will. A computer program that causes delays of several seconds soon comes to seem intolerable to Americans, and thus what at one moment they welcomed as nearly miraculous they soon want to make even swifter.

The sea, even more than the frontier, best explains America's love for invention. Even the pioneers loved the conceit that their Conestoga wagons were prairie "schooners." To push the wooden hull of a merchant vessel into the sea required a substantial investment of venture capital. For many crucial needs, the sea was—and is—America's lifeline. What the sea most impressed upon the American character was a sense of adventure about legal commerce, a zest for business. American business has, ever since, loved nautical metaphors.

It is no surprise, then, that the 5 percent of the world's people represented by the population of the United States raises more than half of all the world's venture capital. Moreover, this proportion masks an even more important reality: Most of the venture capital of Europe and Japan (the other major sources of such capital) is devoted to the reorganization of older firms. But 70 percent of venture investments in the United States is poured into new technologies and new firms. Characteristically, Europeans expend most of their venture capital on less risky mature firms—only 6 percent in new industries. As *The Economist* notes, "When it comes to starting companies and helping young ones grow, America's venture capitalists have *more than half the world's market:* a quarter of that last year was in Silicon Valley alone."[12]

Information technology—now revolutionizing the way business is done and the way the world thinks and acts—will soon become the largest industry of the United States, the industry in which the United States leads by the largest margin, and the industry into which ever new investments of American capital are being poured.

Furthermore, in America, almost everybody is an investor[13]—nearly a third of the adult population—, whereas in Europe most investment comes from banks, not private individuals. Most bankers are content with safe investments. "The notion of investing in ten different companies, hoping to make a killing on the one that survives, is alien to their culture,"[14] says *The Economist.* To venture capital firms, it is the bread of everyday life.

Americans have pioneered in the development of institutions for turning small companies into large ones. Venture capital firms, the first of these institutions, are typically quite small, consisting of a half dozen or so senior partners. These partners are rarely content merely to invest funds. Instead, they identify good people and put in place sound managerial systems to make sure that their investments go toward a successful firm. Typically, they stay with a firm three to five years, until it is strong enough to fly on its own.

Corporations grow, too, from the American spirit of creativity and enterprise. Take the example of Jerry

Yang and David Filo: Both were toiling long hours as graduate students at Stanford University when they decided, in order to pass the time and stave off boredom, to put together an online guide to their favorite Internet websites. In 1995, they formed a company off campus—Yahoo!—to enlarge the same project. When Yahoo! stock went public last year, Yang and Filo joined the growing ranks of high-tech millionaires. Fulfilling a typically American civic role, they endowed a chair at Stanford for $2 million dollars, in gratitude to the university for allowing them to use its computers.[15]

The following chapters show how the business corporation has been the voluntary association through which Americans have wrought the economic revolution that changed the world's horizons. America taught the world that "the social question" that wracked the nineteenth century could be dissolved by universal upward mobility. America taught the world that there is no reason why a majority of people ought to be poor, as poor they all had been (all but a tiny few) until the American experiment.

America was the first nation to give its people an inventive, productive, "just, and generous, and prosperous system," as Abraham Lincoln put it, "which opens the way to all—gives hope to all, and consequent energy, and progress, and improvement of condition to all."[16]

Despite this amazing revolution, of world historical proportions, its dynamo—the business corporation—is an understudied institution, especially by scholars in the humanities. The story of American business, Oscar Handlin has written, is a major fact in American history[17]—and it is barely touched by historians. Not only is the full story not told; in the bits and pieces that *are* recounted, the antibusiness biases of historians are an unpleasant fact of life.[18]

This book grew from three lectures on the future of the corporation that I presented in Washington, D.C., from May to November 1996. For that year, research in preparation for this venture was my chief preoccupation.

In outlining a future "theology of economics" in *The Spirit of Democratic Capitalism*,[19] I distinguished among three specializations. The most general specialization studies basic concepts common to all forms of economic life, such as work, scarcity, plenty, poverty, and wealth. The second studies rival economic systems, such as Third-World traditional economies, socialism, capitalism, "mixed" economies, and the like. At the most concrete level, a third specialization studies particular economic institutions, such as corporations, partnerships, unions, cooperatives, collectives, and so on.

Concerning this third level, in 1981 I published *Toward a Theology of the Corporation* and the proceedings of a summer institute called *The Corporation: A Theological Inquiry*.[20] Thus, in 1996 I was at first reluctant to return to that subject. But I was at last persuaded that much had changed during those fifteen years; that a new abundance of books and articles had begun to fill the long-existing vacuum Professor Handlin had decried; and that the subject deserved fresh scrutiny.

Preliminary investigations showed me that the drama of the corporation was indeed strikingly different at the close of the century from what it had been at the end of the 1970s, before the electronics and communications revolutions. For the business corporation, a new world is in the making. My reflections on that future follow.

The core principle guiding my thought on the corporation, here and in earlier work, has been that business is a serious vocation, open both to moral and to immoral behavior.[21] Much good can be done through business, but much evil, too—even if not as much evil as can be done, and has been done, at the hands of the State. Yet it is not only the *history* of business that has been neglected by scholars but also the *philosophy* of business—the basic analysis of what economic action is; how business practices differ in their structure from (say) artistic practices; and what the particular nature of the business corporation *is*. Thus, in approaching the question of the business corporation, I have devoted a considerable amount of time to clarifying some basic conceptions and, I hope, to raising some deeper issues for further study.

The three public lectures I gave in Washington were well attended, the questions were many and sharp, and C-Span videotaped and played two of them on the air, engendering substantial mail. In the final text, I have had the opportunity to include material suggested by some of these respondents, and they all have my thanks.

I chose the subjects and order of the lectures myself.

First, some reflections on the history and distinctive nature of the business corporation, as a primary institution of democracy (second only to religion); as a necessary but not sufficient condition for the success of the democratic project; and as the major material institution of civil society.

The second chapter turns to the animating force and dynamic drive that gives birth to the business corporation, "the fire of invention," and in particular to the nature of patents and copyrights and some of the perplexities that attend them today, especially in the field of genetics.

Third, I turn to newly agitated questions concerning who ought to govern the business corporation, and in which structures of governance.

For philosophers and theologians, the business corporation raises many fascinating—and so far barely explored—questions. Having entered into these new territories, I can only hope that future generations of humanists will press ahead further, and do better. I guarantee them that they will experience plenty of intellectual excitement and that the results of their investigations will be of great interest to many who toil in the field, too busy sometimes to set down on paper the many things that they know, wonder about, doubt, or would like to pursue further if they could.

Business, born in invention, is an arena of great intellectual ferment. I encourage my colleagues in humanistic studies to plunge into the arena.

· 1 ·

THE FUTURE OF THE
CORPORATION

The war of 1848–1989 between capitalism and socialism is over; capitalism has won.[1] As an *economic* idea, socialism has been defeated. As a *political*
idea, socialism lives.

Almost everywhere, from Chile to Britain, Socialists
have openly embraced private market economies, innovation, enterprise, and economic growth, but they
have not ceased being Socialists. They have not ceased
hating capitalism or assaulting Thatcherism and
Reaganism.

Nor have they ceased identifying their primordial
enemy as the private business corporation. They no
longer speak of replacing the "anarchy" of markets
with national planning, of nationalizing private industries, or of confiscating profits. Today they speak
of environmentalism, of education, of enhancing
human capital, and—to tame their chief nemesis and
rival—of corporate responsibility and corporate governance.

Without going so far as the British journalist Will

Hutton and his big book of 1995, *The State We're In*,[2] British Prime Minister Tony Blair has recently announced his "big idea" for Britain's future: "the Stakeholder Society." *Stakeholder* is intended as a contrast to *shareholder*. Hutton's new big idea is in effect to turn business corporations into adjuncts of the welfare state, in which every citizen of Britain has a stake and on which each citizen has a claim. Everyone in Britain will be a stakeholder. The whole island will "regain" the feeling of belonging to a great family with a corporate purpose and corporate pride. The wallets of shareholders will, of course, be open to other stakeholders.

This is but one example of the new ethos into which the business corporation, like a proud and full-sailed man-o'-war flush with victory, is unguardedly sailing. Another example, closer to home, appears in *Newsweek*'s cover story, "Corporate Killers," featuring mug shots of four chief executive officers.[3] American business, in particular, is being rudely awakened, just at a moment of triumph.

From having been universally mocked as recently as five years ago for falling behind the Japanese and the European Community, American business (manufacturing, in particular) has once again become celebrated for being the world's leader, the system most to be studied and imitated.

Having been accused of being too blinkered by the drive for short-term performance, it has again seized the lead in fields of long-term significance such as biotechnology, telecommunications, and the Internet, in all of which the enormous long-range investments undertaken in the 1980s are at last coming to fruition. And significant productivity increases are beginning to show up in the rapidly expanding service sector, as well.

So why, then, the current rude awakening?

The Achilles' heel of American corporations has been a lack of ideological self-consciousness. Business leaders underestimate the size, intensity, intelligence, and commitment of the forces determined to undermine corporate independence.

Making a business work is not a merely theoretical matter; it takes a tough, confident, and pragmatic mind. Yet in these days of instant communications and easy demagoguery, corporate leaders who lack an unclouded philosophical picture of where they and their opponents stand have too weak a radar to detect the threats arrayed against them. Pragmatism today demands philosophical sophistication. The new sin against pragmatism is to be ideologically naked against determined enemies.

Recently, for example, several British companies signed off on an assertion that

> those companies which will sustain competitive success in the future are those which focus less exclusively on shareholders and financial measures of performance—and instead include all their stakeholder relationships in the way they think and talk about their purpose and performance.

Do the executives of NatWest, Cadbury Schweppes, Guinness, Midland Electricity, Unipart, and other signatories of this report (ominously called "Tomorrow's Company") truly believe that shareholders around the world will continue to invest in companies that so diffuse their purposes? No doubt, being pragmatic gentlemen, they intend to grant the opposition a victory in rhetoric, while afterwards hoping to muddle through more or less as always. One does have the eerie feeling, though, that British companies are letting themselves be led to slaughter like British cattle. Alas, American executives also sign grand manifestoes on the environment and other pieties, thus committing acts of ideological appeasement that in politicians they would speedily denounce.

It is necessary to begin by going back to basics.

What Is a Corporation?

No single factor describes why capitalism emerged; . . . as well as geography, technology and Christianity, a particular form of political and economic system was needed, [which] contained an implicit separation between economic and political power, between the market and government.

ALAN MACFARLANE
The Culture of Capitalism[4]

In the most recent figures (1995), there were nearly 11 million business corporations in the United States, approximately one for every twelve workers.[5] They cover a vast range of types. Some of them are only one-person professional corporations. Some are independent franchises of large chains such as McDonald's, Tastee Freez, Kentucky Fried Chicken, and True Value Hardware. Others are auto dealerships or owners of buildings. One of the largest sources of U.S. jobs, the construction industry (employing 4.5 million), is divided into nearly 600,000 different firms, often involved in quite strenuous local competition and in many market niches. Nearly four thousand business corporations are publicly traded companies, most (but not all) listed on the New York, American, or NASDAQ stock exchanges; these are the companies on which we shall concentrate.

A notable fact about the largest and most famous corporations, the *Fortune* 500, is that they now employ only a little over 9 percent of all U.S. employees, whereas twenty years ago they employed nearly 19 percent (in 1975, 16 million out of 86 million jobs). This decline occurred both because the U.S. economy has created some 50 million new jobs since 1975 and because the largest corporations have shed nearly 4.5 million jobs (from about 16 million to about 11.5 million). Sometimes this shedding happens because firms new to the top 500—such as Microsoft (9,000 employees)—employ as many as 100,000 fewer workers than those they replace.[6]

Thus, the corporation, legally considered, is a

magnificent social invention, prior in its existence to the modern nation-state. The laws governing corporations appear to go back in their origin to ancient Egyptian burial societies and, in the Christian West, to religious monasteries, towns, and universities. Such legally constituted societies possessed an independence recognized by successive political regimes. Their independence from the state had a legitimacy implicitly founded in primeval rights of association and common respect for the sacred. Such institutions were constituted to endure beyond the lifetimes of their founding generation.

The founder of Western monasticism, St. Benedict (480–547), having learned from the early Christian hermitages in Egypt, wisely provided for regular and frequent changes of leadership in each monastery according to formal rules. He staked out unsettled and often remote lands on which the economic sustainability, however meager, of each new foundation could be ensured for generations.

Among historians, it is no longer unusual to suggest that the Benedictine (and other) monasteries sweeping north into Europe from Italy and east from Ireland, gradually beginning to sell their wines, cheeses, brandies, and breads from region to region, were the West's first transnational corporations. The monks introduced to many formerly nomadic peoples what was, for its time, scientific agriculture, thus enabling entire regions to advance beyond subsistence living. From the surplus thus accumulated, libraries and schools, music halls and commissions for paintings grew; civilization took root. Arts and sciences such as botany, metallurgy, and architecture were nourished, and industries such as mining and engineering were furthered. As the historian Paul Johnson has described it:

A great and increasing part of the arable land of Europe passed into the hands of highly disciplined men committed to a doctrine of hard work. They were literate. They knew how to keep accounts. Above all, perhaps, they worked to a daily timetable and an accurate annual calendar—something quite alien to the farmers and landowners they replaced. Thus their cultivation of the land was organized, systematic, persistent. And, as owners, they escaped the accidents of deaths, minorities, administration by hapless widows, enforced sales, or transfer of ownership by crime, treason and folly. They brought continuity of exploitation. They produced surpluses and invested them in the form of drainage, clearances, livestock and seed . . . they determined the whole future history of Europe; they were the foundation of its world primacy.[7]

Thus, contemporary studies of economic history push the origins of capitalism, especially in its underlying institutional forms and laws, back into monastic history, the transnational sensibility of the Christian faith, and the vigorous (if sometimes misguided and invariably controversial) efforts of the papacy to maintain, even by force of military might, the common trade routes and civilizational ties of a united Europe. It is not by accident that the Medal of Europe, awarded annually for contributions to European civilization, bears the embossed portrait of St. Benedict.

Under Islam, by contrast, it is not easy to maintain a separation of church and state; it seems to be part of the essence of Islam, in some sense, to insist on unity. Islam calls for a sort of integrism of faith and life foreign to American Protestantism—but also foreign to medieval Catholicism. When St. Ambrose of Milan (340–397) forbade the soldiers of Emperor Theodosius to enter his cathedral, and they obeyed, he was marking off the boundaries of civil society—in this case, the church—across which the state dared not intrude.[8] In an analogous way, other corporations of civil society appealed to legal precedents, traditions, and principles to defend their own independence from soldiers of the regime, tyrants, and armed bullies who coveted their goods. Often rights *were* lost, injustices *were* done, and right had to be revindicated by force of arms or after the passage of evil times. But a sense of the limits of the state gradually took hold, and with it, the preeminence of the institutions of civil society over those of the state.

Ancient charters, privileges once conferred for exceptional services, exemptions hard won, freedoms achieved, rights recognized by successive regimes, custom, tradition, precedent—in all these, great social power long dwelt. By these means, as well as by experiment, observation, and the common sense of things, the common law developed, especially in Britain. Friedrich Hayek argues that by this evolutionary path the principles of the market economy were learned "not through the design of some wise legislator but through a process of trial and error,"[9] thick with the experience of daily life.

Surely, this is how individual markets grew— among weapons makers, how practitioners came to recognize, for example, good metal from poor, real craftsmanship from shoddy, superior technologies from inferior, models of stunning proportion and form from those merely useful. Tacit rules grew up in such individual markets concerning certain practices that were unacceptable, certain materials beneath approved standards, certain designs recognized as faulty.

Over time, and especially closer to our own time, discoveries such as double-entry bookkeeping, the stock association, mutual insurance societies, the beginnings of organizational theory, patent and copyright arrangements, the power of newly invented machines, and the possibilities of large-scale and mass production opened up new horizons for the business corporation.

Capping these historical developments, the Japanese sociologist Kazua Noda writes:

The corporate form itself developed in the early Middle Ages with the growth and codification of civil and canon law. . . . The first corporations were towns, universities, and ecclesiastical orders. They differed from partnerships in that the organization existed independently of any particular membership; but they were not, like modern business corporations, the "property" of their participants. . . . By the 15th century, the courts of England had agreed on the principle of "limited liability": "If something is owed to the group, it is not owed to the individuals nor do the individuals owe what the group owes." . . . As applied later to stockholders in business corporations [this principle] served to encourage investment because the most an individual could lose in the event of the firm's failure would be the actual amount he originally paid for his shares.[10]

Business corporations—either independent of the state or commissioned by the state (the latter at first more common)—were designed to continue beyond the life of the founding generation, began to provide goods and services on a scale theretofore unseen, and needed vast amounts of human and financial capital. These voluntary associations had to prove themselves, often against quite entrenched opposition from the social classes they threatened (the landed aristocracy, for example). And yet, as Karl Marx noted, they transformed the world. They were indispensable to making it free and prosperous. Yet from the beginning, long before Marx appeared on the scene, business corporations had enemies.

For centuries, men of commerce had been ill thought of by farmers and fishermen, landowners,

aristocrats, churchmen, poets, and philosophers—
seen as pursuers of mammon, middlemen who bought
cheap and sold dear, sophisticates and cheats, huck-
sters, admirers not of the noble but the merely useful,
men with the souls of slaves, cosmopolitans without
loyalties. The counts against them are as old as portions of the Bible, Plato and Aristotle, Horace and Cicero.[11] Aristocrats most businessmen certainly were
not. It is a curious but also crucial fact that men of
business have been morally assaulted, for many generations now, both by the aristocratic and the humanistic Right and by the modern Socialist, social democratic, and merely progovernmental Left. Elites on
both sides denounce them, chiefly on moral (but also
on aesthetic) grounds. When critics reluctantly discover that most of what businessmen do is legal and
moral, and even useful, they retreat to thinking it un-
lovely. Anticapitalism is a far, far darker dye than socialism, and harder to remove.

While it is true that business leaders have few pretensions of being aristocrats or literary intellectuals or
social reformers—not, at least, through their work in
business—it is important to say that business is a
morally serious calling. Through business you can do
great good or great evil, and all the variations on the
scale. But if you do good, you have the advantage that
it is the design of business as a practice and as an
institution that you do so;[12] whereas if you do evil, it
is because you have twisted a good thing to your own
evil purposes and have no one to blame but yourself.

The market may make you or break you, favor your new product or leave it on the shelf—the market does not smile on everyone alike—but in moral matters one is never in a position to say, "The market made me do it." You did it. You are the agent in the market; the market is no agent.

In the early Middle Ages, in sum, the corporation began as burial societies, then monasteries and towns and universities. Implicitly rooted in rights of association, the corporation was "an instrument of privilege and a kind of exclusive body, tightly controlled by the state for reasons of its own."[13] But, as Oscar Handlin points out, in the infant United States there was great resistance to dependence on royal charters from far across the ocean and a great desire among citizens to form corporations on their own to meet innumerable needs. The citizens of Massachusetts, for example, as early as 1636 made up a charter of incorporation for Harvard University, much to the shock of violated royal prerogative on the other side of the Atlantic. Thus, by 1750, while England still had but two universities, the American colonies had six. By 1880, there were more universities in the state of Ohio than in all of Europe combined. Similarly, the railroad had been invented in England, but ten years later there were more miles of railroad in the United States than in all of Britain—and all of Europe—combined.[14] When American lawyers did not even know how to write up proper incorporation papers, they nonetheless did so, and business corporations multiplied up and down the Eastern seaboard. As Handlin has written:

> In 1800 the United States was only beginning its history as an independent nation. It was an underdeveloped country, primarily agricultural, with a population of perhaps 4 or 5 million along the Atlantic coast. Already, however, the United States had more corporations, and more explicitly business corporations, than all of Europe put together; this is an astounding circumstance if you look at it from the point of view of the economist.

Thus, in the United States, the business corporation came into its independent own. Here were born the very first manufacturing corporations in the world.[15] Here corporations ceased being based on state privilege, monopoly, trust, or grant and became inventions of civil society and independent citizens. The state retained a right to *approve of* applications and to register them, for good legal order, but it did not create a right or convey its own power to the corporation or guarantee the latter's survival. The corporation, to survive, could no longer depend on its privileges; it could survive only if it met the needs of its customers and the purposes of its investors. It brought to civil society not only independence from the state but also unparalleled social flexibility and a zest for risk and dare.

Thus, the business corporation grows out of a long,

worthy, and civilizing history. It is a voluntary association committed to a common enterprise—an enterprise association, as Michael Oakeshott would call
it[16]—that consists in providing particular goods or
services to the larger human community, either to the
whole world or to one or more of its smaller communities. The business corporation springs from the creative act of its founders, who are usually moved by a
new invention or idea to provide to a particular market something otherwise unavailable, or not available
in the unique form in which they have presented it.
Their aim is to provide this good or service at a price
attractive to potential customers, in the hope of making a sustainable profit over time.

This hope of a reasonable return on their investment attracts investors to join their funds to the purposes of the firm. As Peter Drucker has pointed out,
in our time shareholders play a more transient role in
the corporation than they have in the past; but for any
growing, creative, and self-transforming firm, new
shareholders willing to invest remain important members of the business corporation:

> Though we have largely abandoned it in legal and po-
> litical practice, the old crude fiction still lingers on
> which regards the corporation as nothing but the sum
> of the property rights of the individual shareholders.
> Thus, for instance, the president of a company will re-
> port to the shareholders on the state of "their" com-
> pany. In this conventional formula the corporation is

seen as transitory and as existing only by virtue of a legal fiction while the shareholder is regarded as permanent and actual. In the social reality of today, however, shareholders are but one of several groups of people who stand in a special relationship to the corporation. The corporation is permanent, the shareholder is transitory. It might even be said without much exaggeration that the corporation is really socially and politically *a priori* whereas the shareholder's position is derivative and exists only in contemplation of law.[17]

Will Hutton's view notwithstanding, the shareholder, however indispensable, is far from the center of things and is likely to be as diffused throughout civil society as the holders of pension funds.

The Corporation and Civil Society

From the point of view of civil society, the business enterprise is an important social good for four reasons. First, it creates jobs. Second, it provides desirable goods and services. Third, through its profits it creates wealth that did not exist before. And fourth, it is a private social instrument, independent of the state, for the moral and material support of other activities of civil society.

In recent decades, this last-mentioned independence from the state has been more and more compromised, through "command and control" regulations and heavy-handed "guidance" from ambitious politicians, promiscuous with state and federal power. Not surprisingly, economic growth has been grinding to slow, fitful levels. And the iron of state programs is rubbing through the fabric of civil society.

Alexis de Tocqueville wrote that religion is the first political institution of civil society.[18] No doubt, Tocqueville had in mind the importance of the truths enunciated by Judaism and Christianity concerning the immortal value of every single person and the crucial role of truth (that is, the opposite of relativism) in making possible the reasoned discourse on which civilization depends. In the opening lines of *Federalist* No. 1, Alexander Hamilton appeals to the capacities of his readers for reasoned argument, pointing out that the upcoming vote on the new Constitution will afford a test of whether, for the first time in history, a nation can be founded not on force or chance, but on reflection and choice.[19] Apart from a prior commitment to truth, no such reflection and reasoned argument are possible; nor is it possible to defend claims to the imperishable rights of humans. (For to claims made on the basis of relativism, not truth, an objector may retort, "That's just your opinion.") To put Tocqueville's point in a contemporary idiom, religious liberty is the first of all human rights, for it implies the dignity and sacredness of human conscience.

Nonetheless, in another sense business is also the first political institution of civil society. Our founders believed it to be part of their originality to establish here a "commercial republic,"[20] because they believed that a republic finds a safer foundation on commerce than on the aristocracy, religion, or the military. A commercial republic has its own temptations, of course, of which neither they nor Tocqueville was unaware (see *Federalist* No. 6). But temptations inherent in other possible foundations are far more dangerous and lack compensating advantages. Following Montesquieu, they held that commerce inherently cries out for law and teaches respect for law; benefits by peace and is destroyed by war; teaches prudence and attention to small losses and small gains; softens manners; diverts attention from issues of glory and spiritual divisiveness to seek modest progress on humble but useful matters; and distributes the practical interests of people, even in the same families, among different industries and different firms.[21]

This last contribution, in turn, affords two advantages: it teaches people even in the same family to understand different occupations, interests, and points of view and how to accommodate them, and it makes it socially far more difficult to form a tyrannical majority. Our founders well knew that the greatest of all tyrants is not a single ruler but an unchecked majority. Democracies in the past, they knew, most often fell because of the tyranny of a majority, and this fate they were committed, by as many remedies as possible, to prevent. The promotion of manufacturing and commerce was a most central and important preventive measure.

Moreover, sources of private capital and private

wealth, independent of the state, are crucial to the survival of liberty. The alternative is dependence on government, the opposite of liberty. The chief funder of the many works of civil society, from hospitals and research institutes to museums, the opera, orchestras, and universities is the business corporation. The corporation today is even a major funder of public television. Absent the financial resources of major corporations, civil society would be a poor thing, indeed.

Pittsburgh, Chicago, New York, Boston, Tulsa, San Francisco, and other American cities—without the philanthropic habits of their corporate leaders over many generations—would be culturally and aesthetically far less pleasing than they are. Most of the buildings on our college and university campuses, even those that are part of state systems, were funded by private donors. What at Oxford and Cambridge monarchs and princes have done is done in America by men and women of business. People in other countries, lacking such traditions, have no way of envisioning the civic leadership, cultural imagination, and immense benefactions contributed by business firms to American life. The magnitude of business and other private giving to colleges and universities in America has no parallel on this planet.

Finally, it should be observed that the ownership of publicly owned companies extends through more than half the American adult population. The largest holders of stocks and bonds are the pension plans of workers, in the public sector as well as the private sector.

To cite just two examples, TIAA-CREF, the pension plan of educators, researchers, and university staffs, as of the end of 1995 owned over $69 billion in stocks and bonds, and the pension plan of the public employees of California owned over $50 billion.

More than 51 million Americans, in addition to those who own stock through pension funds, also own stock either directly or through their personal mutual funds, IRAs, and defined-contribution pension plans. Total stock owned directly by individuals at the end of 1995 was worth $3.6 trillion.[22] Seventy percent of families owning such stock have annual incomes under $75,000. Even apart from new investments, current funds may be expected to grow, on average, at about 8 percent a year. The independence of families from government is closely tied to such investments.

If in the near future social security is privatized, pouring multiple billions of dollars of new funds into productive investment, the independence of individual families will be mightily fortified. Shareholders are no small, narrow band of the American population but a large majority.

Business corporations are crucial institutions of civil society—they support research, the arts, universities, charities, and good works of many kinds, and they undergird the financial hopes of American families. Above all, they expand the space for independence and private action in the public sphere. They add greatly to the diversity of sources of public imagination, initiative, and experimentation.

The Stakeholder Society

From these reflections it is obvious that the business corporation is indispensable to the maintenance of any true experiment in self-government. It plays a crucial role in the design of the republican experiment—it is the commercial part of the commercial republic, the principal economic part of political economy. In that sense, then, all citizens of the republic have a *stake* in the success and vitality of American corporations. From these derive Americans' financial independence from government and their practical freedom of action.

Here a fateful equivocation must be cleared up. The word *stakeholder* has two senses. The term derives from the time of the Homestead Act, when Americans heading West could take out a claim on a parcel of land and be guaranteed the ownership thereof by the protection of the state.[23] The federal government sponsored this act for two reasons: first, to make sure that the West developed as free states, not slave states, and second, to reap the benefits of a regime of private ownership and private practical intelligence. At that time, Americans believed (in lessons derived from the experience of ancient Rome and Greece as well as from medieval Europe and Britain) that the common good is better served by a regime of private property than by common ownership or state ownership. They further believed that more intelligence springs from a multitude of practical-minded owners of their own property than from a prestigious body of planners, however brilliant. Iowa, in effect, would develop with more practical good sense under scores of thousands of small owners than under a plantation system such as that of the South or some scheme of state planning.

In this context, *stakeholder* means *owner* and private *risk taker.* The purpose of an arrangement of society into many private stakeholders is to secure the *general* welfare and the larger *public* interest. The stakeholder society in this sense is the very foundation of the free society. Maintaining it entails investment, hard work, responsibility, risk, and earned reward or, often enough, personal failure. Freedom is tied to risk and responsibility.

The social democratic sense of the term *stakeholder* is quite different. Stakeholders are all those who deem themselves entitled to make demands on the system and to receive from it. A Britain, for example, imagined as a "stakeholder society" is one in which each citizen is entitled to make claims on others according to his or her needs. These needs are infinitely expansive, however, so perpetual dissatisfaction is guaranteed. No conceivable amount of security or health care can satisfy human beings; our longings are infinite, beyond all earthly satisfaction. If today's ten most dangerous diseases are conquered, the next ten will rise to cause new anxiety. A stakeholder society is bound to be like the nest of open-mouthed chicks. The link between the desire to receive and personal responsibility never forms.

The social democratic dream has many of the characteristics of a religion. It is, in particular, the dream of a united national community, conferring on all a sense of belonging and participation and being cared for. In practice, of course, things work out quite differently. Its schemes of social belonging usually end up with populations far too accustomed to receiving and demanding. Those most skilled at mobilizing demands fare best. While social democracy speaks the language of community and compassion and caring, the reality is original sin, that is, socialized self-interest. Social democratic societies are not notably happy or contented societies.

In the social democratic context, a stakeholder is a claimant on the public purse. From a social democratic perspective, the stakeholder in the traditional sense, the true owner and bearer of responsibility and risk, is called a "mere shareholder" and is accused of having a "pinched," "narrow," and "selfish" view of society. To paraphrase George Santayana on Puritans, a social democrat cannot bear to see self-reliant, responsible, prospering, and independent institutions without wanting to put them in state-directed harness.

The paradox of socialism is that it actually results in the opposite of its hopes: an unparalleled isolation of individuals from the bonds of personal responsibility and social cooperation.[24] In an obverse paradox, while extolling the language of community and social sharing, social democracy necessarily excites envy, a social passion worse than hatred, and it inevitably divides citizens into factions that make on the state unceasing claims of favor, entitlement, and privilege. Each faction jealously and militantly claims its own "just" stake. Thus, social democracy dampens ambition, imagination, personal independence, individual risk taking, and economic creativity; it nourishes a society of clients, supplicants, and demanders of rewards; and it aspires to a relative uniformity of condition among those whose stakeholding amounts to what Hayek aptly called serfdom. Eight score years ago Tocqueville also foresaw this effect:

I am trying to imagine under what novel features despotism may appear in the world. In the first place, I see an innumerable multitude of men, alike and equal, constantly circling around in pursuit of the petty and banal pleasures with which they glut their souls. . . . Over this kind of men stands an immense, protective power which is alone responsible for securing their enjoyment and watching over their fate. That power is absolute, thoughtful of detail, orderly, provident, and gentle. It would resemble parental authority, if, fatherlike, it tried to prepare its charges for a man's life, but on the contrary, it only tries to keep them in perpetual childhood. . . . It gladly works for their happiness but wants to be sole agent and judge of it. It provides for their security, foresees and supplies their necessities, facilitates their pleasures, manages their principal concerns, directs their industry, makes rules for their testaments, and divides their inheritances. Why should it not entirely relieve them from the trouble of thinking and all the cares of living?[25]

That is not a stakeholding society. That is serfdom.

The End of the Republican Experiment?

As the first streaking fingers of the twenty-first century rise toward dawn, there is no guarantee that the republican experiment will not perish from the face of the earth. The dream of social democracy, which would replace the republican idea, still bewitches many minds. Social democrats today claim to be converted to markets, private property, and contemporary (rather than nineteenth-century Marxist) economics. But of course they mean *bridled* markets, *socially responsible* private property, and *government-managed* economics. As Will Hutton puts it: "Keynesian economics is best."[26] They cling to their dream; it assures them of moral standing, indeed superiority.

In the American republic, both the economy and religion are purposefully kept separate from the state. Yet there is no way to keep the wall of separation between economy and state as high as it is between church and state; this is so for two reasons. First, although the supply of money could theoretically and advantageously be privatized, as Friedrich Hayek[27] has urged, we have long lived under a consensus that the government, through the relatively independent Federal Reserve Board, ought to maintain public control over money. Second, the workings of business, founded on private contracts under the rule of law, demand the involvement of government in the making and enforcement of corporate law.

But this asymmetry between religion, in which "Congress shall make no law," and business, to which the making and enforcing of law are indispensable, makes it even more important for business leaders to be philosophically vigilant—that is, *principled* and unrelenting against the trespasses of government power on private property.

At this point, commercial habits such as a mere deal making and a mutually agreeable pragmatism are self-mutilating. Business leaders must be careful not to give away the store—and they must insist on deadly seriousness in the use of key words such as *stakeholder.*

Will Hutton, for example, proposes eight major changes in British law, mandating eight sets of controls on procedures of corporate governance.[28] What he cannot stand is the firm's independence: "The firm is a law unto itself, sovereign of all it surveys. Its only job is to succeed in the market place." He makes "succeed in the market place" seem easy, trivial, frivolous—when British firms, like all others, are struggling to survive in global competition. And he makes even a limited sovereignty over oneself (under "the laws of nature and nature's God")—that is, liberty understood as self-government—seem like an abuse rather than the inner dynamism and goal of all human history.[29] Hutton takes no count, finally, of the burdens his eight proposals would pile onto the already inadequate shoulders of the regulatory bureaucracy, and no count whatever of the costs in animal spirits, inefficiency, bureaucratic overlay, excessive record keeping, poor morale, and feelings of pointlessness his "reforms" would entail.

His American counterparts are worse. Professor Ralph Estes, American University proponent of the Stakeholder Alliance and author of *Tyranny of the Bottom Line: Why Corporations Make Good People Do Bad Things*, also thinks keeping a sound bottom line is easy, so he wants to add a dozen or so other lines. For him, stakeholders "include employees, customers, neighbors and communities, financial investors, suppliers, and the greater society." Not just the Great Society, note, "the *greater* society"—"all who are affected significantly by the enterprise." Are all these persons to be asked to pay the corporation for tangential benefits they receive from it? Oh no. They are supposed to exact new costs from it:

> The scorecard has to be enlarged to incorporate effects on all stakeholders. It must record the workplace injuries, pollution emissions, product liability claims

and settlements, recent layoff and plant closure data, indictments, fines by and settlements with government regulators. Indeed, it must record the information necessary for stakeholders to make informed decisions in the marketplace, the way the 1930s securities acts required reports that would permit financial investors to make informed decisions. And this information must be publicly available, in an annual Corporate Report to Stakeholders supplemented as necessary by ad hoc disclosures. With disclosure, stakeholders have the information they require to make informed economic decisions and can then regulate corporate behavior.[30]

American Labor Secretary Robert Reich, for a time the voice of Europe in America, also hectored corporate leaders, proposing the use of tax favors to steer corporations in directions social democrats favor.[31]

As the strongest private institutions standing in the way of the administrative state, business corporations are certain to be the unceasing target of the frustrated and almost desperate energies of the Left. Nearly all welfare states are broke or in most serious deficit. Many dependent populations are demoralized and living half lives rather worse in matters of the spirit than those of earlier generations of the poor (among whom so many of us were born), who at least felt independent and proud. In improving the lot of the elderly and in some forms of social insurance, the welfare state has had some sound successes that the party of liberty ought not to disparage but to defend. Nonetheless, in all the giant administrative states in our time, the new soft despotism has been experienced long enough and is coming to be hated.

In this age in which the welfare state is broke and in deficit, where then will the social democrats turn for plunder? The famous Willie Sutton robbed banks because that's where the money was; that, apparently, is where his near-namesake Will Hutton got the idea—in Hutton's case, robbing not banks but business corporations. He wants to leave their private property, risk taking, and free markets intact—only to regulate them, harness them, and guide them so his team gets the fruits they want, willy-nilly. (See the appendix.)

It is time, then, for public enemy number one, the business corporation, to take account of its own identity, its essential role in the future of self-governing republics, and its central position in the building of the chief alternative to government: civil society. The corporation is what it is and does what it does; but it is an invention of free people, not a cold meteor fallen from the skies. It has changed often in history and, by its very self-discipline, inventiveness, and creativity, has surmounted even greater threats than it faces today. Now, however, it will need a greater degree of philosophical and public policy self-consciousness than ever before. The corporation has some serious external enemies and some serious internal flaws—for example, in the procedures that lead to excessive compensation at the top, to excessive insecurity at all levels, to anomalies of self-governance, to turmoil about patents. The business corporation is once again in a fight for its life, and the sooner the dangers that menace it are exactly discerned, the better.

Consider this first chapter a version of that old, famous telegram: "DISASTER STOP LETTER FOLLOWS."

· 2 ·

THE FIRE OF INVENTION,
THE FUEL OF INTEREST

On a cold winter day in February 1859, in Jacksonville, Illinois, Abraham Lincoln delivered a "Lecture on Discoveries and Inventions," in which he described, since the time of Adam, six great steps in the history of liberty. The last of these great steps, Lincoln held, is the law of copyrights and patents. His lecture gives the best account I have ever read of the reasons why the United States, in a brief Constitution of barely 4,486 words, includes a clause guaranteeing the "right" of inventors and authors to royalties for patents and copyrights (the single mention of the term *right* in the body of the Constitution). Until I read Lincoln on this point, I had never encountered anyone who gave patents and copyrights such high importance.

On that cold February day on the Illinois prairie, you must imagine Lincoln, tall and gangling, gazing across the stove-heated room, with a sweep of his hand summoning up a vision of that first "old fogy," father Adam:

There he stood, a very perfect physical man, as poets and painters inform us; but he must have been very ignorant, and simple in his habits. He had no sufficient time to learn much by observation; and he had no near neighbors to teach him anything. No part of his breakfast had been brought from the other side of the world; and it is quite probable, he had no conception of the world having any other side.[1]

By contrast with this naked but imposing Adam, able to speak (for he names the animals) but without anyone to talk to (for Eve "was still a bone in his side"), Young America, Lincoln notes, the America of 1859, is awash with knowledge and wealth. Whereas the first beautiful specimen of the species knows not how to read or write, nor any of the useful arts yet to be discovered, "Look around at Young America," Lincoln says in 1859. "Look at his apparel, and you shall see cotton fabrics from Manchester and Lowell; flax-linen from Ireland; wool-cloth from Spain; silk from France; furs from the Arctic regions, with a buffalo robe from the Rocky Mountains." On Young America's table, one can find

> besides plain bread and meat made at home . . . sugar from Louisiana; coffee and fruits from the tropics; salt from Turk's Island; fish from New-foundland; tea from China, and spices from the Indies. The whale of the Pacific furnishes his candle-light; he has a diamond-ring from Brazil; a gold-watch from California, and a spanish cigar from Havanna.

Not only does Young America have a sufficient, indeed more than sufficient, supply of these goods, but, Lincoln adds, "thousands of hands are engaged in producing fresh supplies, and other thousands, in bringing them to him."

The Grand Historical Adventure

Here, then, is the question Lincoln poses: How did the world get from the unlettered, untutored backwoodsman of the almost silent and primeval Garden of Eden to great cities, locomotives, telegraphs, and breakfast from across the seas? He discerns six crucial steps in this grand historical adventure.

The first step was God-given: the human ability to build a language.

The second step was the slow mastering of the art of discovery, through learning three crucial human habits—observation, reflection, and experiment—which Lincoln explains this way:

> It is quite certain that ever since water has been boiled in covered vessels, men have seen the lids of the vessels rise and fall a little, with a sort of fluttering motion, by force of the steam; but so long as this was not specially observed, and reflected and experimented upon, it came to nothing. At length however, after many thousand years, some man observes this long-known effect of hot water lifting a pot-lid, and begins a train of reflection upon it.

Given how arduous it is to lift heavy objects, the attentive man is invited to experiment with the force lifting up the pot lid.

Thousands of years, however, were needed to develop the habit of observing, reflecting, and experimenting and then to spread that art throughout society. Some societies develop that habit socially, and some do not. Why, Lincoln asked, when Indians and Mexicans trod over the gold of California for centuries without finding it, did Yankees almost instantly discover it? (The Indians had not failed to discover it in South America.) "Goldmines are not the only mines overlooked in the same way," Lincoln noted. Indeed, there are more "mines" to be found above the surface of the earth than below: "All nature—the whole world, material, moral, and intellectual—is a mine; and, in Adam's day, it was a wholly unexplored mine." And so "it was the destined work of Adam's race to develop, by discoveries, inventions, and improvements, the hidden treasures of this mine."[2]

The third great step was the invention of writing. By this great step, taken only in a few places, spreading slowly, observations and reflections made in one century prompted reflection and experimentation in a later one.

The fourth great step was the printing press, which diffused records of observations, reflections, and experiments in ever-widening circles, far beyond the tiny handful of people who could afford handwritten parchment. Now such records could be made available to hundreds of thousands cheaply. Before printing, the great mass of humans

> were utterly unconscious, that their *conditions*, or their *minds* were capable of improvement. They not only looked upon the educated few as superior beings; but they supposed themselves to be naturally incapable of rising to equality. To immancipate [sic] the mind from this false and under estimate of itself, is the great task which printing came into the world to perform. It is difficult for us, *now* and *here*, to conceive how strong this slavery of the mind was; and how long it did, of necessity, take, to break it's [sic] shackles, and to get a habit of freedom of thought, established.

Between the invention of writing and the invention of the printing press, almost three thousand years had intervened. Between the invention of the printing press and the invention of a modern patent law (in Britain in 1624), less than two hundred.

The fifth great step was the discovery of America. In the new country, committed to liberty and equality, the human mind was emancipated as never before. Given a brand-new start, calling for new habits, "a new country is most favorable—almost necessary—to the immancipation of thought, and the consequent advancement of civilization and the arts." The discovery of America was "an event greatly facilitating useful discoveries and inventions."

The sixth great step was the adoption of a Constitution, in which the word *right* occurs only once, and that in Article 1, section 8, clause 8—the recognition of a natural right of authors and inventors. Among the few express powers granted by the people to Congress, the framers inserted this one:

> To promote the Progress of Science and useful Arts, by securing for limited Times to Authors and Inventors the exclusive Right to their respective Writings and Discoveries.

The effect of this regime was not lost upon the young inventor and future president.

"Before then," Lincoln wrote, "any man might instantly use what another had invented; so that the inventor had no special advantage from his own invention." Lincoln cuts to the essential: "The patent system changed this; secured to the inventor, for a limited time, the exclusive use of his invention; and thereby added the fuel of *interest* to the *fire* of genius, in the discovery and production of new and useful things."

"The fuel of *interest* added to the *fire* of genius!" Ever the realist, Lincoln knew what is in the human being: to be a genius is one thing, to be motivated is quite another, and then to be supported in this motivation by a wise regime is an unprecedented blessing. By contrast, a regime that does not secure natural rights depresses human energy.[3] Natural rights are not mere legal puffs of air; they formalize capacities for action that in some societies lie dormant and in others are fueled into ignition.

The United States, Lincoln believed, lit a fire to the practical genius of its people, among the high born and the low born alike, wherever God in his wisdom had implanted it. In the same year as his lecture, 1859, Lincoln himself won a U.S. patent, number 6469, for a "device to buoy vessels over shoals." That patent is not a bad metaphor for the effect of patents on inventions: to buoy them over difficulties.

The great effect of the patent and copyright clause on world history was a remarkable transvaluation of values. During most of human history, *land* had been the most important source of wealth; in America, *intellect* and *know-how* became the major source. The dynamism of the system ceased to be primarily material and became, so to speak, intellectual and spiritual, born of the creative mind. Lincoln's motive in favoring the Homestead Act and the patent clause (and both together) was to prevent the West from being dominated by large estates and great landowners, so that it might become a society of many freemen and many practical, inventive minds. And so it has. More than 5 million patents have been issued in the United States since the first patent law of 1790.[4]

From Lincoln to John Paul II

Implicit in Lincoln's Jacksonville lecture are several assumptions about the nature and meaning of the

universe. Lincoln saw history as a narrative of freedom. He believed devoutly that the Creator of all
things had made human beings in his own image—
every one of them, woman and man—to be provident.
History, he thought, is the record of how human beings have gradually come to recognize their true better
nature and striven to make it actual, both in their own
lives and in the institutions of their republic.

Thomas Jefferson wrote that "the God who gave us
life gave us liberty,"[5] and, while Lincoln did not actually say that our God wishes to be adored by men who
are free, he sacrificed much, very much, so that in
1861–1865 this nation might have "a new birth of
freedom." That horrifying bloody project, he held—
40,000 dead and wounded in a single day (and more
than once)—was willed by God. The universe is so
created that it positively calls forth human freedom.
To that call, it is the sacred duty of humans to re-
spond, even at enormous cost.

Some seven score and two years after Lincoln's lecture in Jacksonville, there came an international echo
of his beliefs from an unlikely quarter, in a worldwide letter published by Pope John Paul II in Rome,
on May 1, 1991, *Centesimus Annus*. I do not know
how much of Lincoln Pope John Paul II has read, but
there is no mistaking the Lincolnian wavelength on
which the papal letter on political economy traveled.
His mind sweeping history like Lincoln's, and noting
that for thousands of years *land* was the primary form
of wealth, the pope writes: "In our time, in particular,

there exists another form of ownership which is becoming no less important than land: *the possession of know-how, technology and skill.*" The wealth of the world's most economically advanced nations is based far more on this type of ownership than on natural resources.

"Indeed, besides the earth," observes the pope, "man's principal resource is *man himself.* His intelligence enables him to discover the earth's productive potential and the many different ways in which human needs can be satisfied." The pope's words seem cousin to Lincoln's sentence, "All nature—the whole world, material, moral, and intellectual—is a mine," and "the destiny of Adam's race" is "to develop, by discoveries, inventions, and improvements, the hidden treasures of this mine."

This thought is picked up later by the pope:

> Whereas at one time the decisive factor of production was *the land,* and later capital—understood as a total complex of the instruments of production—today the decisive factor is increasingly *man himself,* that is, his knowledge, especially his scientific knowledge, his capacity for interrelated and compact organization, as well as his ability to perceive the needs of others and to satisfy them.[6]

Similarly, where Lincoln had written "but Adam had nothing to turn his attention to [but] work. If he should do anything in the way of invention, he had first to invent the art of invention," the pope writes:

At one time *the natural fruitfulness of the earth* appeared to be, and was in fact, the primary factor of wealth, while work was, as it were, the help and support for this fruitfulness. In our time . . . work becomes ever more fruitful and productive to the extent that people become more knowledgeable about the productive potentialities of the earth and more profoundly cognizant of the needs of those for whom their work is done.[7]

Washington, Madison, and Lincoln held that the American regime, measured by "the Laws of Nature and Nature's God," would blaze a trail for other nations. Under Pope John Paul II, important portions of its "new science of politics," after much testing, have at last been ratified by what is now the most widely held body of social thought in the world.[8] In the coming third millennium, this practical intellectual influence may stand as an important contribution of American civilization to world history.

In this new era, observes Fred Warshofsky, a journalist-historian: "Creativity, in the form of ideas, innovations, and inventions, has replaced gold, colonies, and raw materials as the new wealth of nations." The remarkable "new technologies, new processes, and new products that constitute intellectual property now form the economic bedrock of international trade and national wealth."[9] As more and more nations take halting steps on the path of democracy and free markets, they will increasingly need the fire of invention, the fuel of interest.

Some Clarifications

Having sketched the theological horizon within which the law of patents and copyrights functions in world history, we must now come down to practical questions. First, a clarification: the concepts of *copyright* and *patent* are not the same and have separate histories. The early and somewhat shadowy origins of the first tentative laws of patents lie in seventeenth-century Britain and in Germany and France; but these were often in the form of "grants of privilege," of monopoly or favor, awarded by the crown.

As Lincoln noted, the invention of the printing press in 1456 forced the issue of copyright on the attention of authors and philosophers, notably (in the English world) Hobbes and Locke. To the monarchs, copyright laws had early commended themselves as a means of censorship; but against this, philosophers and poets (like John Milton) soon enough rebelled. In addition, writers and inventors came increasingly from the lower ranks, from persons not of noble birth, who had no inheritance to prop them up, and were dependent on their wits for their livelihood. They wanted financial independence from printers, publishers, church, and crown.

In the United States, under the leadership of General Charles Pinckney of the South Carolina state legislature, that state put in place a law protecting the patents of inventors in 1784. The year before, 1783, under the leadership of James Madison, Virginia had already passed a law protecting the copyright of authors. These two events may explain why at the Constitutional Convention (on Saturday, August 18, 1787), Pinckney submitted a minute to the drafting committee urging the inclusion of a clause protecting patent rights, while on the same day Madison submitted another protecting copyrights.[10] Apparently, there was little serious debate; by 1787, all the states except Delaware had adopted similar legislation, and all the delegates were intent on promoting the sciences and useful arts in the infant republic as a whole. Both minutes were usefully combined in a single clause and given a place of honor among the enumerated powers in Article I.

By the time of the U.S. Constitution, the rooting of copyright in the common law and natural rights was already beyond dispute.[11] U.S. laws, however, clarified that the right inhered in the individual creator, not in the state, and is not a privilege or favor extended by the legislature. The law, instead, was regarded as securing a preexisting right (as the general verb used in the Declaration of Independence, "to secure these rights," clearly expresses). Thus, only in America were patent and copyright laws given constitutional status, and only here, for several generations, were they widely and popularly appealed to by rich and poor alike.

Now for the definitions. *Copyright*, literally, is a right to make copies, and a *patent* is a right to own royalties to a novel product or a novel process.

Copyrights protect the creations of writers and artists, whereas patents protect the inventions and discoveries of inventors. Paul Goldstein of Stanford puts it quite succinctly: "Copyright is the law of authorship and patent is the law of invention." He adds:

> Copyright protects products of the human mind, the thoughts and expressions that one day may be found on the pages of a book and the next in a song or motion picture. . . . Patent law's domain is invention and technology, the work that goes into creating new products, whether tractors, pharmaceuticals, or electric can openers. The United States Patent Act gives an inventor, or the company to which he has assigned his rights, the right to stop others from manufacturing, selling, or using an invention without the patent holder's permission.[12]

Not everyone accepts this concept. The philosopher Tom G. Palmer, for example, denies that there can be property ownership in ideas; ideas are "ideal objects," he says, quite different in their characteristics from material things.[13] But Palmer does not do justice to a crucial point: patent and copyright laws do not protect ideas or concepts, considered in their immateriality and shareability. On the contrary, copyright laws protect the concrete expression of ideas, their incarnation in the precise particulars of language and song singled out by their creators. Similarly, patent laws protect the concrete reduction to physical practice of practical insights. In both cases, it is not the general idea that is protected but the concrete incarnation.

For one to obtain a copyright, for example, it is not enough to claim novelty for an idea or concept. The artistic product must originate with the author—be original in that sense—but it need not be novel. To qualify for protection under copyright laws, a creator must provide an embodiment in particulars, a unique expression of an idea that many might otherwise possess in a generalized way. In the case of patents, novelty is crucial, but here the inventor must supply a concretely practicable embodiment that shows precisely how the general idea may be put in practice. The concreteness of the creation qualifies it for protection, not the spiritual immateriality of the general idea.

Let me repeat, since so many fail to grasp it on one pass: a *patent* covers a practical insight reduced to practice—that is the trick of the thing, the hard part— and a *copyright* covers the unique, personal way of presenting something by a writer or an artist. A patent is closely linked to the inventor's concrete grasp of the distinctive advance he or she makes on the practical state of the relevant art. A copyright is very clearly linked to the personal subjectivity of the author. Here concreteness is all, and, as the legal theorist Wendy J. Gordon points out, this concreteness furnishes the necessary analogy between property rights in material things and property rights in highly

personal expressions of ideas (copyrights) or concretely exercisable practices (patents).[14]

Finally, we must clarify the rationale of the emphasis of the laws on proof of novelty. Some think it irrational that two or more persons may come to substan-
tially the same invention while filing for a patent a
day apart. It is unfair, they say, to reward the one
totally and deny the other totally.[15]

But this is to forget that it is characteristic of any
extension of the rule of law into new territory—the
Homestead Act, for example—to reward those who
stake the first claim. This may not be a perfect system,
but tradition has proved its workability. The law sets
up a competition for the frequent provision of real
benefits to the common good of the society. Since for
this purpose novelty is prized, timing is of the essence.
As Professor Gordon sharply puts it, "When several
scientists are hot on some trail, a promise of exclusiv-
ity to the winner may be the only prize meaningful
enough to keep the race from flagging."[16] While the
law must be as fair as humanly and administratively
possible, it cannot play the role of an omniscient
judge. We await perfect justice in a different city.

Five Disputed Questions

Even in the midst of the most terrible civil war in
history, Abraham Lincoln assiduously promoted both
the Homestead Act and the Land Grant College Act

and continually praised the patent and copyright clause, stressing the importance of practical intellect to the generation of the nation's wealth.[17] Considering the high importance that Lincoln attached to this issue, it is odd to discover the relative neglect of intellectual property by scholars and social philosophers. Although the literature is already vast—in the past decade, more work has appeared on "intellectual property" than on "property" in general—countless serious issues remain unresolved. For this reason, the American Enterprise Institute not long ago commissioned a short survey of yet unanswered questions, Robert P. Benko's *Protecting Intellectual Property Rights.*[18]

The necessary inquiries, Benko shows, cut across several different disciplines. Many historical questions have gone uninvestigated. The philosophical foundations of patents and copyrights stand in considerable confusion. Still unresolved are the economic aspects of these laws, both in precise economic concepts and in their empirical foundation. It goes without saying that lawyers argue about their foundations, meaning, and implications. Very few political theorists have given to patents and copyrights anything like the importance that Lincoln attached to them. Lincoln saw that the free society must open up economic opportunity to all, especially at the bottom, and that for this purpose, public encouragement for invention and discovery is critical. Few other thinkers have seen in these laws a crucial foundation of the free society as Lincoln did.

Furthermore, one finds in the academy today many who deny that there are such things as "rights," and even some who treat rights as they treat unicorns.[19] Similarly, one finds a surprising number who attack even the concept of patent and copyright. A surprising number of the latter actually have difficulties with the prior concept, property rights. They find property rights too "conservative" and implicated in something they affect to despise: "possessive individualism."[20] Others dislike the seeming anomaly of granting "temporary monopolies" and thus stigmatize patents and copyrights with the contempt traditionally attached to monopolies.

This, of course, is a terminological mistake. *Monopoly* belongs to the language of domination over competition, but *copyright* belongs to the language of private property and establishes a right to enter into markets. The point of a monopoly is to extinguish competition, but the point of protecting the copyright of authors is to ignite competition. The recognition of copyright increases the number of competitors; its aim is the opposite of monopoly.[21]

Again, while some hate the lack of competition that inheres in what they improperly call "temporary monopolies," others would prefer, at least with regard to intellectual achievements, an altogether noncompetitive world. Some even prefer a world of common ownership.[22] (This appeal to ownership shows that they, too, are thinking of a "property" right, not a "monopoly.") These critics further forget that existing patents and copyrights often inspire new rounds of competition to "go around" the existing claims, with the hope of launching more successful creations. This is especially true in medical and pharmaceutical research.[23] Patents and copyrights do not end competition; often, their success inspires it in surrounding areas.

Finally, truly serious practical problems in the field of patents and copyrights today arise in three areas: first, the search for international protections for intellectual property; second, the search for protection in the new environment of electronic and digital communications; and, third, moral qualms about the awe-inspiring fields of genetics and biogenetics.

Regarding international law, I offer two remarks. Most nations have had no Lincoln to clarify their thinking about the central role of intellectual property in the creation of wealth. In many countries, therefore, basic philosophical clarity is lacking. Moreover, even where such clarity is achieved, the institutional and administrative requirements for staffing a national patent and copyright office are beyond the abilities of many nations. A large number of international institutions must be confronted (the World Intellectual Property Organization, World Trade Organization, and UNESCO, not to mention bilateral and multilateral boards and commissions), and finding one's way through that minefield is not easy. (It takes more than a village—it takes hundreds of thousands of dollars and many thousands of man hours—to win an international patent today.) While most of the political debate and jostling on the subject focus on WTO rules, enforcement proceedings, bilateral treaties, and jawboning, these are really just manifestations of the lack of consensus on the foundations of intellectual property. More sharply put: if developing and non-Western nations *did* appreciate the importance of patents and copyright, then international conventions and enforcement would be straightforward—as routine as international enforcement of business contracts, tangible property rights, and maritime law, where there is already consensus.

Regarding the grievous problems for patents and copyrights brought on by new modes of communication, I make but one observation. Since the printing press occasioned the emergence of copyright laws in the first place, wouldn't it be ironic if a new communications revolution—this time in electronics—rendered copyrights unprotectable?[24] For myself, I propose a simple rule: never bet against the survival of the book, the printed word, and the copyright.

Again, some people say that 50 percent of the computer software put into individual work stations is already being copied in violation of copyrights. (In borrowing a program from friends, is there anyone without sin?) But, as Philip E. Ross has recently shown, in the war between inventors seeking to protect their intellectual property and "pirates" struggling to swipe it, the battle is constantly shifting fronts. Two broad strategies for combating piracy are shaping up: one technological, the other legislative. Both hardware and software are being developed that can "read" copyright signatures to block illegitimate copying and "encrypt" envelopes that must be decoded before use. On the other front, legislators have already imposed a "royalty tax" on copying materials and recording devices at the point of sale to compensate those who will lose profits from their use.[25] With appropriate skepticism about their practicality, we can anticipate other such legislative initiatives in the future.

Finally, profound philosophical and theological questions are also raised by patenting in genetics and biogenetics, and I must say a few words on these matters because of their urgency.

But Isn't Genetics Different?

The prospect of "patents on body parts" (that is the way discussion of genetics is amateurishly put) seems to arouse revulsion, for example, in a writer whose article I once published as an editor.[26] As a philosopher and theologian, however, I have come to have a higher professional regard than I used to for what my colleague James Q. Wilson calls "the moral sentiments,"[27] including spontaneous revulsion. For a long time, I resisted formulating philosophical views rooted in the sentiments, and I still deplore how people say,

"I *feel* that" instead of "I *judge* that." Nowadays, however, since to be politically correct we are supposed to make ourselves believe a dozen revolting things before breakfast, we have all learned to take spontaneous feelings more seriously than we used to. Revulsion is often reason's best defense.

True enough, medical inventors in our time have developed magnificent artificial substitutes to replace certain "body parts" after our original organs and limbs give out, enabling us to live longer and better lives. When Pope John Paul II broke his hip in 1994, for example, a partial hip replacement was available for him.

In genetics and biogenetics, however, something rather different is in question. Nobody is talking about physical body parts such as arms, legs, and kidneys but about identifying and isolating components of our genetic makeup. This "something different" is so intimately bound up with our personal identity that we are bound to approach it with awe, not a little trembling, and caution. Research in this area arouses deep but obscure feelings. There is strong resistance to the idea of patenting important elements of the human person—characteristics that are, as it were, right at the inner trunk of the tree of family traits that shape each of us. How can it be right to patent something so intimate, so potent, and so surrounded with danger? Genetic research would seem to give human beings power over the genetic makeup of future generations. Isn't that too awesome a power to give to humans?

Despite such fears, practically everyone agrees that there can be a good side to some genetic research. On the positive side, here is Pope John Paul II:

> Scientific progress such as that involving the genome is a credit to human reason, for man is called to be lord of creation, and it honors the Creator, source of all life, who entrusted the human race with steward-ship over the world.[28]

But what about the potential evils, the "Franken-stein" effects? Richard D. Land and C. Ben Mitchell mention several:[29] the creation of "transgenic ani-mals," that is, human-altered creatures genetically engineered to serve as means to other ends;[30] the pat-enting of genetically engineered human beings;[31] and even the prospect of human embryos cloned for the sole purpose of "farming" their tissue for medical re-search.[32] The first of these cases, transgenic animals, disturbs some scholars, but others find it not much different from the use of genetics in altering plants. As for the other two—genetically engineered human beings and the cloning of embryos for "farming" pur-poses—they arouse profound moral doubts, even moral revulsion, in many.

Before we collapse all problems into these worst cases, however, it is useful first to distinguish among the many types of genetic research. Certain diseases and bodily vulnerabilities, it has long been known, are inherited, and the precise genes that result in these defects can now be isolated. At earlier stages in medical history, medical interventions to cure or to temper inherited diseases and other vulnerabilities have been regarded as ethically permissible, even admirable.

For healing such difficulties, for example, this new knowledge about genes and how to isolate them, although it has yet to cure anyone of a genetic disease, has opened up new possibilities for intervention. That intervention is more radical, it is true, but it does not alter the fundamental structure of the human person; its main goal, on the contrary, is to rectify abnormal deficiencies. The isolation of the gene causing sickle cell anemia, a grave blood disorder affecting more than 50,000 Americans (most of them African-American), has led to the development of a synthetic molecule that shows great promise in treating the inherited disease. Similar molecules may provide remedies for cystic fibrosis and other diseases.[33] The pope himself lauds this sort of genetic medicine:

> We can reasonably foresee that the whole genome sequencing will open new paths of research for therapeutic purposes. Thus the sick, to whom it was impossible to give proper treatment due to frequently hereditary pathologies, will be able to benefit from the treatment needed to improve their condition and possibly to cure them. By acting on the subject's unhealthy genes, it will also be possible to prevent the recurrence of genetic diseases and their transmission.[34]

Genetic research leading to pharmaceutical interventions of this type would seem, then, to fall within traditional ethical norms.

Morally serious people must soon develop a complete taxonomy of the types of genetic research and genetic interventions and the different sorts of ethical reflection each type might call for. The entire subject is new and arduous. The key point to be established for now is that there are different types of genetic research, each requiring its own proper form of ethical analysis. To speak of genetic research globally, without making important distinctions about kinds and specified differences, is a serious error. After we have considered the evidence, it is important for us to reach moral judgments early in this new field, but according to the ancient motto: *Festina lente* (hurry slowly).

We can never forget that medicine as practiced by two recent totalitarian regimes, Nazi and Communist, fell into grievously immoral uses. Such uses of medicine (or of scientific research more generally) need to be identified as early as possible and blocked in the body politic by appropriate checks and balances. But sinister uses—that is, *abuses*—of sound medicine should not be confused with beneficent uses. While the use to which genetic research is put must be subject to ethical judgment and command, the gaining of the required knowledge and the learning of the required practice would seem to be ethically good, analogous to the acquisition of practical knowledge in other areas of human inquiry.

For, in the timeless philosophy *(philosophia peren-nis)*[35] of the Western tradition, the human mind has as its natural good the raising and answering of all questions about everything, the complete fulfillment of the unlimited hunger to know. For me, this tradition was well expressed by my Jesuit teacher in Rome many years ago, Bernard Lonergan:

> Deep within us all, emergent when the noise of other appetites is stilled, there is a drive to know, to understand, to see why, to discover the reason, to find the cause, to explain. Just what is wanted, has many names. In what precisely it consists, is a matter of dispute. But the fact of inquiry is beyond all doubt. It can absorb a man. It can keep him for hours, day after day, year after year, in the narrow prison of his study or his laboratory. It can send him on dangerous voyages of exploration. It can withdraw him from other interests, other pursuits, other pleasures, other achievements. It can fill his waking thoughts, hide from him the world of ordinary affairs, invade the very fabric of his dreams. It can demand endless sacrifices that are made without regret though there is only the hope, never a certain promise, of success. What better symbol could one find for this obscure, exigent, imperious drive, than a man, naked, running, excitedly crying, "I've got it"?[36]

Granted, then, that some forms of genetic research are morally sound, even imperative, even while other forms may finally be judged to be evil, why should we allow such knowledge to be patented? Don't patents serve private interests rather than the common good?

Does a Patent Regime Protect Private Interests or Public Good?

On my way to answering this question, I hit a real stumbling block in the words of an author from whom I had learned much about intellectual property and, indeed, about property rights of all kinds, Friedrich Hayek. In short, much to my initial surprise, Hayek *opposed* patents and copyrights:

> I doubt whether there exists a single great work of literature which we would not possess had the author been unable to obtain an exclusive copyright for it. . . .
>
> Similarly, recurrent re-examinations of the problem have not demonstrated that the obtainability of patents of invention actually enhances the flow of new technical knowledge rather than leading to wasteful concentration of research on problems whose solution in the near future can be foreseen and where, in consequence of the law, anyone who hits upon a solution a moment before the next gains the right to its exclusive use for a prolonged period.[37]

Hayek usually turns out to be right, so at first these sentences made me hesitate. After reflection, however, I found that I must part company with Hayek on this matter.

One alternative to a patent system is research that is kept secret—a regime of "trade secrets." There are thousands of such private and closely guarded trade secrets, the most famous perhaps being the formula for Coca-Cola. But the great advantage of a regime of patents over a regime of trade secrets is open publication. A patent is placed on the public record in precise detail; only that which is declared in public documents is protected. Ironically, therefore, a regime of patents makes publicly available the practical knowledge that a regime without patents often leaves secret and inaccessible and thereby expands the realm of publicly accessible science.[38] Further, it adds to the drive to inquire the incentive to better one's condition. This, as Lincoln saw, is an unstoppable combination.

The other alternative to a regime of patents was suggested by Hayek, who argued that the case for copyright "must rest almost entirely on the circumstance that such exceedingly useful works as encyclopaedias, dictionaries, textbooks and other works of reference could not be produced if, once they existed, they could freely be reproduced."[39] (Take, for instance, the fact that Noah Webster was one of the great early defenders of copyrights in the United States.) Except for that case, and contrary to his views on other forms of property, Hayek seemed to approve of common ownership of intellectual property.

Yet a regime of common ownership, often advanced as fulfilling the ideal of equality, would impose a cruel inequality on creators and inventors. These socially valuable persons would be expected to bear the costs

in time, effort, financial investment, and personal sacrifice necessary to produce their creations, while all
others would be freeloaders. Nations that have protected patents and copyrights, experience shows, have
seen an explosion of invention and discovery far beyond anything achieved under nonpatent regimes. Although the Soviet regime made enormous investments
in education, scientific research, and technological experimentation and although it produced some real
successes, it lagged far behind in advancing the public
good of its citizens and produced very little by way of
practical invention for the common good.

While recognizing that intellectual property rights
set certain temporary limits on consumption (by li-
censing the number of producers), I believe that with-
holding intellectual property rights limits production
far more drastically, as the case of the Soviet Union
clearly shows. This leads to the decisive point: how
can anything be consumed if it has yet to be produced,
and how can it be produced if there is no incentive for
inventing it and bringing it to market?[40] Moreover, as
Edmund W. Kitch points out in a remarkable paper,
the fact that invention is treated as a property right—
like a prospector's right in mining—establishes a market mechanism that gives clear signals about which
inventions to bring forth first. Here, as elsewhere,
these market signals greatly improve the efficiency of
inventiveness[41] and call forth extraordinary efforts
from ordinary people. Thus, well-designed regimes
may bring forth better fruits than their citizens could

produce unaided and thus stir strong feelings of gratitude among their citizens for the blessings they impart.

There is a second advantage to patent regimes: the expenses of research and the costs of applying for patents (and these have become formidable) are borne mostly by inventors. Of course, those companies that depend on a steady stream of a few successful inventions need to pass along the costs of their unsuccessful experiments; in this sense, they often "write off" these costs under research and development. Only if an invention actually succeeds in the market—and this happens in no more than a small fraction of cases—does its inventor recoup these expenses;[42] in fewer still does he make a profit. The costs of failure are by and large paid by luckless inventors, who may expend vast resources and come up empty—only to blaze the trail for those who follow in their footsteps and learn from their failures.

It is often suggested, finally, that the protection of intellectual property benefits the rich nations at the expense of third world countries. Why should rich "fat cats" prevent poor "copycats" from making cheap versions of certain pharmaceuticals or software programs? Or why, as James Boyle asks in a new book from Harvard University Press, should rich "first world" buyers be allowed to execute a "ferocious intellectual land grab" in the third world by enforcing rights to intellectual property?[43] This argument ignores the fact that those who are most victimized by the lack of intellectual property protection are the poor, as four considerations show.

First, when their best inventors and most creative minds migrate to countries where patent and copyright laws hold sway (like the many Russians now working in the American computer industry), nations without such protection suffer brain drain. Second, venture capital is desperately needed in the developing world, but the absence of intellectual property laws scares away venture capital—and jobs. Third, without patent and copyright protection, it is unlikely that multinationals will set up shop in a particular country; yet multinationals tend to bring with them more benefits, more humane treatment, and greater opportunity than are usually found in local sweat-shops.[44] Fourth, without the protection of intellectual property rights, indigenous industries are unlikely to grow into multinational income producers and large-scale employers of the sort their nations need.

Conclusion

Sound public policy since at least the time of Aristotle's *Nicomachean Ethics* has clung to a forthright maxim, verified in practice over and over again: "If you want more of something, reward it; if you want less of something, punish it."[45] Regimes without patents penalize inventors and reward freeloaders. Patent regimes recognize the right of inventors and authors to the fruit of their own labors as a right in common law. They do so because this right serves the common good by stimulating useful inventions and creative works from which a grateful public benefits. Far from protecting private interests at the expense of the common good, patent protection advances the common good by means of private interests. The common good is the end; private interest is the means. Finally, experience shows that a patent regime serves the common good better than any known alternative.

The Jewish and Christian Bible, Abraham Lincoln's favorite book, taught him that it is often among the humblest things of this world that the greatest blessings lie hid; and that it is among things disdained and held in low esteem, among things overlooked and undervalued, that the greatest treasures often lie. Lincoln put this beautifully: "All nature is a wholly unexplored mine." Thus, patent and copyright laws, seemingly minor and humble instruments of liberty, were celebrated as never before by that both humblest and greatest president of the United States.

This lowly constitutional principle, one of the half-dozen most decisive advances in the history of liberty, gives incentive to millions to look again at the humble things around them, to discern the secrets the Creator has hidden from eternity for the benefit of all his people, if only the bold, the persevering, and the diligent will strain to uncover them.

· 3 ·

ON CORPORATE
GOVERNANCE

Like a proud frigate, the American business corporation is sailing confidently into the twenty-first
century. But a cannonade has already erupted off
port, and off starboard, rockets' red glare, bombs
bursting on "corporate governance" and "economic
fairness." The corporation—the most successful institution of our time, flexible and adaptable beyond all
others, maintaining its way in whitecapped seas while
others founder—is suddenly a ship that others want
to capture. They want to reform it into something it is
not. There is a lot of ruin in today's cries for reforming
corporate governance.[1]

Most of today's reformers are quite sophisticated.
They are no longer socialists, they say. They want to
"humanize" the corporation, not to expropriate it.
Some even quote a passage Adam Smith wrote about
the corporation in 1776, well before the nineteenth
century arrived. Smith feared that the corporation,
that then-new beast, slouching toward who knows
what city, that oddly contrived thing that separated

ownership from management, could not possibly work. He gave three pretty good reasons why:

> The directors of such companies, being the managers rather of other people's money than their own, it cannot well be expected that they would watch over it with the same anxious vigilance with which the partners in a private copartnery frequently watch their own. Like the stewards of a rich man, they are apt to consider attention to small matters as not for their master's honour, and very easily give themselves a dispensation from having it. Negligence and profusion, therefore, must always prevail, more or less, in the management of the affairs of such a company. It is upon this account that joint stock companies for foreign trade have seldom been able to maintain the competition against private adventurers. They have, accordingly, very seldom succeeded without an exclusive privilege, and frequently have not succeeded with one. Without an exclusive privilege they have commonly mismanaged the trade. With an exclusive privilege they have both mismanaged and confined it.[2]

Adam Smith was analytically clear and prescient; the problems he described dog us still. But as a predictor of the corporation's future, he was uncharacteristically wrong.

Our strategy in attacking the subject of corporate governance is to resolve the question, What *is* the business corporation? and to follow through on its implications in today's unprecedented circumstances.

This will require just over half the chapter. At the end, we need to tackle related problems such as the destructive power of envy, corporate compensation, and the corporate habit of appeasement.

What *Is* the Business Corporation?

Having been the social instrument by which the bourgeoisie, in "scarce one hundred years, has created more massive and more colossal productive forces than have all preceding generations together," the publicly held business corporation is arguably the most successful, transformative, and future-oriented institution in the modern world.[3] It has been far more open, more creative, and infinitely less destructive than the nation-state, particularly the totalitarian state. Face to face with nation-states, churches have necessarily become their rivals, since in the moral sphere states lean to absolutism. But churches have not really had to become rivals to the corporation. For the corporation strives mightily to be compatible with every sort of religious regimen and not to challenge any frontally.

The corporation is by its nature a voluntary and part-time association, with no pretensions of being a total community (with rare exceptions, as in certain Japanese companies of a generation ago).[4]

Nonetheless, this fairly unassuming form of social organization has transformed the world before our

eyes—thrown great silver airplanes into the skies, gir-
dled the ether with invisible webs of instantaneous
global communication, and brought fresh mangoes to
the breakfast tables of the Northern Hemisphere and
crisp, vacuum-packed Wheaties to the Southern.

But what *is* a business corporation? It is so various
a thing that it is not easy to define. In the United
States, the publicly owned business corporation con-
stitutes barely 1 percent of all business organizations.
Unincorporated businesses, partnerships, small corporations, and even privately held giants (such as
Mars, Inc., or Parsons Brinckerhoff, the huge engineering company) outnumber the publicly owned
businesses 99 to 1. Yet this tiny minority of publicly
owned firms produces more than half of America's
economic output.

Moreover, publicly owned businesses come in all
sizes and shapes, from networks of neighborhood
hardware stores to manufacturers of millions of automobiles annually like General Motors and vast,
sprawling energy companies like Mobil, Exxon, and
Shell; from nimble, inventive cocoons of technical
originality and marketing flair such as Intel and Microsoft, to the lumbering, but newly dynamic heirs of
the nineteenth-century, night-whistling Atchison, To-
peka & Santa Fe. You name it, you want it available
to buy, and the likelihood is very great that a corporation is even now making it and looking for you.

So, what was the publicly owned business corporation invented to do? What is its purpose and point?

What type of institution is it? By what standards ought it to be judged? These are crucial questions to resolve, before blindly careening into new forms of corporate governance.

Executive Energy

The great political philosopher Michael Oakeshott distinguished between two generically different types of association, the civic association and the enterprise association.[5] The civic association aims at something larger than any particular end, interest, or good: the protection of a body of general rules and a whole way of life; in other words, the larger framework within which, and only within which, the pursuit of particular ends becomes possible, peaceable, and fruitful. Given such a framework, individuals are free to choose myriad activities. The state is a civic association, he thought, or at least should be; so is the church; and so are many kinds of clubs, charitable organizations, and associations for self-improvement.

Oakeshott did not much like ideologically driven states, parties, or even activists; they narrow down the realm of choice. They falsify the nature and purpose of the state, making it a political party rather than a peaceable society.

By contrast, Oakeshott noted, the enterprise association is built to attain quite particular purposes, often purposes that tend to come around again quite continuously, as restaurants are built to feed people day after day. Enterprise associations are focused, purposive, instrumental, and executive: they fix a purpose and execute it.

Moral standards and standards of civic virtue still apply to enterprise associations, of course. "There is honor even among thieves," the ancient proverb says—but not enough! Enterprise associations that injure the virtue of their members—like states that injure virtue—are objects of shame; consider the Mafia.

On other counts, however, publicly held business corporations are not at all like states, and their self-governance is not at all like that of a national government. These are two very different types of organization. In states, executive power is feared and therefore checked; in the corporation, it is desired and therefore husbanded. In this respect, in fact, corporate governance is perhaps a little like the executive branch of government taken by itself, apart from the judicial and the legislative branches. Like the executive branch, the governance of a business corporation requires a focused unity; there is little room within it for checks and balances.[6] Its point is executive, and "energy in the executive"[7] is its sine qua non. The corporation is not a state; its internal governance is not a state government—these are totally different species of association.

The standards of accountability to be met by the head of a major corporation are far narrower than those facing the head of the executive branch of government. His job description is very different from that of the president of the United States. The president must face democratic elections, itself an odd and not entirely executive measure of performance. The U.S. president must also play the almost kingly role of representing the people in symbol, rite, and performance.[8] Only in the third place does the president play the role of prime minister, that is, political strategist and persuader. Coming in a distant fourth is a U.S. president's role as executive officer of an administration, one of three branches of government. All this is very different from the president of Citicorp, who is selected by a small board and instructed to achieve defined objectives, within a relatively narrow strategic plan laid out by that same board (almost certainly with his input).[9]

Within a corporation, no one should even desire "separation of powers," for the whole point is to create something new, to achieve something, whereas in government the whole point is to prevent leaders from achieving anything beyond the already stated powers and purposes of the union. The reason for checks is to keep in check, and the reason for balances is to keep a balance. In an important sense, not achieving something, not violating the original constitution, is the preeminent aim. Wise persons do not want governments to act until they are carried forward, like rhinoceroses rising slowly from the mud, by the hydraulic force of a very large and durable consensus. But the same wise persons want business corporations to be able to act quickly, even to turn on a dime when they are losing money or when they spot suddenly arising possibilities, to take the risks for which their investors have entrusted them with well-defined executive power.

To repeat, governments move, must move, by consensus—slow as elephants and resistant as donkeys. But businesses must move by executive intention. Without waiting for public consensus—indeed, hoping to be first to reach the market—businesses must move instantly, like pulsing electronic signals. Often they must move by executive will, ready to act even before all the information is available that the intellect might crave.

Investors rightly want business to be effective; they are willing to accept intuition, hunch, and even instinct rather than the qualities they might prefer in other contexts, such as full deliberation and judiciousness, so long as swift action results in more reliable and speedier contact with reality than reflection. The laws of action are not identical with the laws of reflection, and temperaments fitted to the one are not always suitable for the other.

I linger on this point for one reason only. The word *governance* naturally leads the mind to think of *government*. Therefore, discussions of corporate governance tend to be conducted, often unconsciously, in the language of political philosophy, worked out for the government of nations. Such discussions lead to an enormous mistake of logic and language, to a way of thinking not at all appropriate for the governance of business corporations. The problem of business governance is not a problem of political philosophy; it is a problem of business philosophy. (In a similar way, theologians wince when they hear the governance of churches discussed in the language of political philosophy.) Politicians, churchmen, and people in business ask different types of questions, work under certain different rules, and require different types of outcomes; even their manners and styles are different. The general rule is this: for each different type of human activity, its own proper philosophy.[10]

The problem, as Peter Drucker has suggested, is that the philosophy of business is a field waiting to be born. Indeed, Drucker himself tends to speak of "organizational theory,"[11] which sounds a little like sociology rather than a philosophy of business. What we need is in fact a philosophy of business, because it is important to keep clear about what a business is and is not, especially today.

For the American business corporation has been so successful during the past hundred years, particularly during the past fifteen, that many people want to lasso it, break its spirit, and for their own purposes train it to become something else. Charities and helping organizations, for example, want the corporations to pay their upkeep. Heavily indebted and failed welfare states want to bend the corporation to meet the state's own unkept promises. In general, former socialists want to tame the business corporation, make it sit up and dance, perhaps do tricks to music.

As a matter of fact, after the dramatic collapse of the world's leading example of actually existing socialism, the USSR, socialists (and, in America, just plain "progressives"), without ever admitting their errors or correcting their way of thinking, still want to socialize the corporations. But now they want to do it through movements such as environmentalism, the philosophy of "stakeholders,"[12] children's rights,[13] and some forms of feminism and gay rights. And many corporate leaders are still being rolled, played for patsies, and driven forward blindly by their inability to think clearly and make distinctions.[14] Although appeasement seems to be an all-too-common reflex,[15] intellectual cowardice is not strictly required for business success. A sound philosophy is permitted. It must be developed, fortified, and honed to a practical edge not just by philosophers but by corporate doers themselves.

The Ant and the Elephant

What, then, is a business corporation, philosophically considered? From a philosophical point of view, the business corporation is so flexible, practical, polymorphous, adaptable, and various that no organizational definition of its essence is realistic. Most often, the corporation begins with an idea—an invention, perhaps, or simply an insight—around which investors pool their resources with the hope of creating new wealth.[16] But ideas for how to provide new goods or services are virtually infinite in shape and form. A part of a new corporation's originating idea, in fact, may be the conception of a new way of organizing the delivery of goods or services. Gateway Computers and Lands' End are not organized like Hewlett-Packard or Lord & Taylor. Pfizer is not organized like Rexall.

Furthermore, it is a mistake to think that only corporate executives at the large public firms are among the "rich" so widely disdained, at least in public, by leftist congressional and media leaders. The owner of the Ourisman auto dealerships in the Washington area, the retailer, may be wealthier than any executive at General Motors, the manufacturer. Ownership is, typically, a surer road to wealth than employment.

The concept of the business corporation, therefore, is like the magical ocean in the fairy tale, shallow enough for an ant to wade through and deep enough for an elephant to drown in. It must be as pluriform as the goods and services to be provided and the markets in which customers meet providers. It must be able to change with changing times, technologies, political conditions, and moral habits. Its range is not infinite; there are cultures in which it cannot survive and others in which it cannot thrive.[17]

When, under Soviet communism, for instance, economic acts between consenting adults were punishable by death, in effect the private business corporation was in intensive care or dead. Circa 1979, on most of the territory of this planet (China, the USSR, and over other large geographical stretches) private corporations were *verboten*, forbidden, against the law. In many third world countries, epidemics of corruption and dictatorship—like plagues of leeches—bled corporations white and drove many of them out. In short, the corporation is a form of organization that can survive in most sorts of cultures but not in all.

In Adam Smith's day, the business enterprise was essentially a small owner-managed affair. As late as 1820, in all of France there were not more than several dozen business enterprises (or factories) employing as many as twenty persons in one building.[18] As Smith foresaw, the device of splitting ownership from management required by the growth of great stock associations shifted the flows of motives, interests, and passions.[19] When the executive manager was no longer the owner, he was in charge of spending someone else's money. (His compensation may be chiefly in stock ownership, but that does not make him *the* owner—far from it.) He might well feel comfortable with a handsome salary and enjoy the prestige of being boss, while losing the singular mark of the original owner—the willingness to be imaginative and take risks. The original owner, meanwhile, might have qualms about risks taken with his money by new managers, more qualms than he once had about risks he used to take lightheartedly for himself. As a thinker who paid a great deal of attention to men's passions, interests, and motives, Smith may have been the first to worry about future problems of corporate governance. He was not the last.

Why Do Firms Exist?

Why, then, despite Adam Smith's foreboding, do business corporations exist at all? (It once seemed to me that worrying about the existence of God was enough for a theologian, without worrying about the existence of firms.) There are two main reasons why firms exist, first pointed out by R. H. Coase in 1938 in a brilliant gem of an essay, "The Nature of the Firm,"[20] followed by a legion of other commentators including, recently, Richard Posner.[21] First, it may be far more efficient for an economic agent to hire many of the people his extensive activities will involve than to negotiate arms-length contracts with each of them as independent customers or suppliers. Such negotiations would otherwise consume his energies and time, and make day-to-day adjustments nearly impossible.[22] Second, in manufacturing, for instance, the need for capital is immense. Organizing a firm to rationalize, focus, and synchronize diverse economic activities is the most efficient way to attract capital.

In our day, therefore, at least this much can be said in defining the business corporation: it is an enterprise association that depends on the public market for investors willing to invest a portion of their savings in it. It is legally incorporated as a legal person and governed under by-laws and by a duly appointed or elected board of directors. Its purpose is to provide goods and services of a distinctive type (or in a distinctive way) in the expectation of earning profits for its investors, with fiduciary care for the investments entrusted to it. It is the most efficient way yet discovered to minimize transaction costs and attract large amounts of investment capital. The corporation so conceived is the world's best hope for the creation of new economic wealth.

Pirates!

In the 1980s, financiers like Carl Icahn, Michael Milken, and many others began to make an analysis of the problems of corporate organization not unlike that of Adam Smith. They judged that many corporate managers were not doing nearly as well as they could with the value under their stewardship. Armed with new financial methods of their own devising for assembling large amounts of capital, they began buying and reshaping corporations to bring out overlooked values. No good deed going unpunished, these laser-eyed analysts were treated like pirates preying on Spanish galleons that had gold hidden in their holds. "Corporate raiders" they were called—and worse—and they terrorized an entire ocean of slowly moving companies.

Alarmed and awakened, corporate executives and corporate boards began trimming ship and preparing either to repel the Blackbeards or to outsail them. Disapprove of them or not, we owe these "pirates" a debt. They were not alone in issuing a stirring wake-up call—worldwide economic competition arrived simultaneously—but they certainly got everyone's attention.[23]

And they left us with a lingering problem. What if corporate management *is* comfortable and content with "good enough"—or worse? What should be done, and who should do it? All may agree that corporate managers are not the most important owners, only somewhat more so than mere employees—for, even as employees, most of their compensation comes as stock ownership, much of it in options that give them longer-term interests than many ordinary stockholders. But, insofar as they are employees, who is it that really employs them? Legally, it is the board of directors that has that responsibility, along with several other responsibilities, such as the strategic direction of the company and provident forethought about its resources, needs, and future contingencies. But what if the board is in the pocket of, or in collusion with, the corporate managers, some of whom also sit on the board? What if the board loses dispassionate objective distance? Critics have by now developed several lines of assault.[24]

Besides, who *are* the owners of the contemporary corporation? Who are they in whose name the board of directors acts as steward? In a publicly owned company, the rightful owners may be scattered all over the stock market. More likely, though, large portions of the shares of any major company are held by specific mutual funds, pension plans, and other institutional investors, acting as proxies for hundreds of thousands of individual owners, most of whom are likely to be, in the term of art, *rationally ignorant*—that is, poorly informed and willingly uninvolved—concerning an individual corporation's practices and prospects.[25]

Mutual Funds and Pension Funds

In fact, two great changes in the structure of corporate ownership have transformed the environment in which corporations now operate. First, mutual funds today are far more numerous than they were fifty years ago. Second, by now the pension plans of employees, not only private but also public, own nearly 30 percent of the stock of major corporations.[26] All by itself, the pension plan of the California State Public Employees owned $72 billion in assets in 1993, more than the gross domestic product of some member states of the United Nations.[27]

Both the directors of mutual funds and the directors of pension plans want to invest in corporations that produce high returns. They are competing against their peers in seeking higher returns; they demand "performance." Managers of corporations that "perform" admirably year after year become market favorites. As their corporations attract investors, the wealth of their stockholders increases. So does the value of their own employees' pension plans and the value of other pension plans invested in company stock, as does the value of the mutual funds that have selected them for investment.

Thus, when someone writes or says that Wall Street likes or does not like a particular company, we need to remind ourselves that the active intelligence that first reaches such judgments is probably working in a pension plan office in Sacramento or Albany or Eugene, Oregon, or in a new, quick-to-the-draw mutual fund in Denver, Santa Fe, or Fort Lauderdale, or in the small and unpretentious offices of financial legends in Menlo Park or Omaha. Wall Street has been decentralized. One result is that corporate managers dare not become lazy and self-satisfied. They have powerful incentives to seek out untapped resources within their own companies and to turn these to creative use. Money managers all around the country are watching them like hawks, competing with one another to spot hidden strengths or weaknesses before others do.

Moreover, the directors of pension plan funds and other investors have learned by experience that they can, if necessary, vote a chief executive officer out of office by taking over the board of directors of his corporation. They have already done so at GM, American Express, IBM, and Westinghouse. Boards have power to hire and fire, and boards are themselves elected (usually for renewable three-year terms) by stock-holders. Large stockholders cast weighty votes. So large stockholders from pension plans and mutual funds have begun throwing their weight around. (When the directors of state pension plans and mutual funds enter a room, corporate executives have learned what to call them—Ma'am or Sir.)

Looking for the Right Stuff

Conversely, money managers are learning the hard way that their bread is buttered by corporate manag-ers with vision, steadiness, talent, and guts—in short, with what used to be called "the right stuff." That means character, wedded to a precise talent, a talent for figuring out the right thing to do and for doing it the right way and at the right time. Today there are a lot of people competing fiercely to find the few persons in the whole world not only capable of being great CEOs but already in place in the right companies. Corporations are executive enterprises. That is of their essence. In business, the quality of the people in charge determines nearly everything else.

On the brink of the twenty-first century, therefore, the environment within which corporate governance operates is drastically different from what it was even twenty years ago. The performance of CEOs is under much greater scrutiny. Investment flows are instantaneous and worldwide. Moving beyond traditional watchdogs of business such as banks and regulatory agencies, money managers at newly powerful institutions such as mutual funds and pension funds have gained an upper hand over corporate managers through computer-driven tools of analysis and boldly employed voting clout. Today every corporate manager in his right mind knows that his perch is insecure. Unless he is employed by a firm that he himself or his family founded (and not even that will always protect him), he can expect the average length of his tenure to be about that of a linebacker in the National Football League, a little less than six years. He faces very little danger from boredom, laziness, or complacency. What Learned Hand in the 1950s called in a famous monopoly case "the quiet life" is no longer the CEO's lot. He will be lucky to have the freedom of spirit to make time for solitude and soul. He will be lucky not to make a mess of his family relationships, especially with spouse and older children.

A Well-Lighted Place

To summarize the argument thus far: once you grasp the need for energy in the executive and note the new competitive conditions prevailing in the corporate environment, much of the hullabaloo about corporate governance seems radically misplaced. According to most of the analysis, the problem is that of finding checks and balances and otherwise borrowing from the power-limiting institutions of republican government. But the problem of corporate governance is not to check power—that is already done today by unprecedented dimensions of competition—but rather to summon up and channel power. Checks enough abound: the explosion of financial information and analysis—not only in the number of financial television channels, the Internet, and the proliferation of financial newsletters but also in the institutional power of independent professional analysts representing large shareholders—has made the business corporation quite suddenly a well-lighted place.

Thus, what Adam Smith feared about the stock association—that in zeal its managers would be inferior to its owners—is not likely to happen today. In fact, today's publicly owned firms run by hired managers may be far more performance oriented than privately owned and managed firms of yesteryear. There are now many more ways to keep chief executive officers on their toes than there were two decades ago. Investor checks and balances are very strong, indeed.

The great problem of corporate governance today, therefore, is not how to create checks and balances against power. The great problem is how to govern corporations internally to overcome the great cultural tide of envy and "political correctness" that bids fair to swamp them in syrupy, corrosive sentiment.

On Envy: "Thou Shalt Not Covet"

We turn, then, to the perennial and persistent problem of envy and its destructive social power, as well as to auxiliary problems such as corporate compensation and the strategy of appeasement.

Covetousness and envy are permanent and universal passions whose social destructiveness was recognized many civilizations ago, in the time of Deuteronomy, long before there were any business corporations. Universal covetousness and envy are burning embers that never die. Gasoline is thrown upon them today by such lines as these: "Executive compensation is obscene," "Corporate executives live too high," and "Wages of workers decline, while those of top management are growing astronomically." Not much is left for traditional socialists to do today except to fan prairie fires of covetousness and forest fires of envy.

Inequality is the main line of attack because "downsizing," last season's craze in the perpetual assault on corporations, turned out to be exaggerated. Contrary to the impression fostered by the popular media, job stability has been slightly greater in recent years than in earlier periods.[28] The proportion of high-paying jobs has also been dramatically increasing, not decreasing. The corporations listed in the Fortune 500 have fewer employees today than twenty years ago, but a flood of smaller, newer high-tech companies has created a large labor market in high-skilled jobs.

It is quite true, if ironic, that Wall Street responds favorably to notice that behemoths like AT&T are restructuring their work force. Announcements of lay-offs are sometimes met by small jumps in the stock price—sometimes, but not always. What do these positive effects mean? They mean that firms must meet the demands of new technologies and new worldwide competition. It means, further, that there is more value in AT&T than AT&T was previously delivering. (Recall that unrealized value belongs to the pension plans of millions of workers outside AT&T.) Change at AT&T was "overdue." The environment for laid-off workers with skills in communications, luckily, is an up market.[29] Two-thirds of those laid off by AT&T were back at work in three months. With severance, some had, in effect, a paid vacation.

Let us return for a moment to the point that change was overdue. On a recent trip to Chile, a distinguished business leader asked me why American firms wait so long before facing serious problems and then do so in a way so inhuman to their work force. Sometimes, of course, sudden technological change catches firms by surprise. But often, as silently as plaque on teeth, problems are building up even while executives neglect preventive measures. "Overdue change" is usually due to inadequate and tardy "executive energy," not to excessive energy. Much human turmoil might be spared if, on a regular basis, executives summoned up the energy to take countermeasures against inertial growth; preplanned attrition alone might do it.

Isn't it an irony, meanwhile, that leftist journalists and social critics, while becoming ever more skeptical about the desirability of the permanent marriage contract, should expect jobs to be forever? Do they expect employees to receive diamond rings on the day they are hired? In reality, finding good employees and training them is expensive, and mutual loyalty between firm and worker usually helps both. Under sudden layoffs, both suffer.

Incidentally, the fact that accusations about big corporations' "destroying jobs" occur at a time when the U.S. economy has created more than 50 million new jobs (during the past twenty-five years, at a rate of 19 million per decade) is not as paradoxical as it seems. In normal times, big firms are constantly reorganizing as conditions change; sometimes they shed jobs and sometimes they hire steadily. Some creation of new jobs—especially in entire industries never heard of before, such as among new technology companies—takes place in small firms (which by definition virtually all new firms are). And it is precisely by creating many new jobs that small firms become large firms. Many if not most small firms, however, are either suppliers or distributors for, or provide services to, large corporations.[30] The upshot is that a huge proportion of the U.S. labor force flocks like seagulls around the busy places generated by large, complex business organizations, no matter whether those businesses are hiring or shedding.

Two Types of Inequality

Still, the problem of inequality is a serious one, even if a false one. It is a false problem because there is and can be no human system that makes humans equal (in the sense of uniform). It is contrary to human nature even to *wish* to be considered identical to anyone else, replaceable, a cog in a slot. Individuals know they are unique, utterly unlike every other—quite unlike even their twin, if they happen to have one. They have unique ambitions, energy levels, moral strengths, knacks, and luck. Uniqueness, not uniformity, is the human mark.

Equality as uniformity, furthermore, can be socially imposed only through the most vigorous tyranny. The proper name for such a project is not egalitarianism but *egalityranny*. This project, in effect, lops off heads, slices off feet, and reduces the length of arms and fingers to a standard size. As such, equality-as-uniformity is antihuman. It is quite different from equality-as-uniqueness, which demands equal respect precisely for what is unequal (not uniform) in individuals.

This commonsense observation collides with two persistent facts. One is the universality of the human passions of envy, covetousness, and the desire to cut one's betters down. The other is that, in any democracy, many people resent the flaunting of differences of station, as if these represent a lapse into aristocratic privileges, a violation of democratic sensibilities. Both these facts—universal envy and democratic resentment—feed the boa constrictor that squeezes "equality" into "uniformity."

Unthinkingly, the flaunting of class differences does at times emanate from corporate board rooms, corporate parking places, corporate dining rooms, corporate jets, and other indiscreetly managed corporate perks. This is a serious fault. In democracies, corporations need to practice an unpretentious, open, man-in-the-street style at every level of the firm, or else they will awaken resentments in a democratic populace.[31]

Obviously, two further tendencies pull firms in opposite directions. Certain signs of status are inevitable, expected, and socially beneficial. Others are not. Some forms of recognition are offered in lieu of a raise. In any sound organization, superior achievement should receive superior recognition, and symbolic forms of recognition seem relatively costless. The trick, however, is not to allow differences in class status to arise between management and workers. This subject deserves often-renewed attention, for as marketing and sales departments well know, status pleases more than money, is eagerly sought and greedily devoured.

Nonetheless, wrongly signaled status is socially

destructive. You cannot build community, teamwork, or a sense of family across fissures of rigid class consciousness. Ordinary folks want to believe that all class boundaries are permeable, if not by themselves, then in the person of their bright sons and daughters. The corporation needs to convey the air of being upwardly open. Alas, some corporate board rooms seem designed to impress, to exclude, perhaps even to exude a hint of the baronial. I do not say that this is always wrong; but it is, unless countered in other ways, a great danger to the system as a whole.

For the moment Americans begin to think that class lines are being drawn, bile rises in their bellies. Management and labor need to share a similar world of upward mobility, of achievable status, of belonging to the same team. They must do so in fact, and they must appear to do so. The tendency to forget this—among union leaders, as well as managers—is universal and perennial, so it must be consciously combated. (Union leaders also face special temptations: to become confrontational in order to be viewed as "fighters" for their members.) In a democracy, an upwardly mobile, achievement-oriented, shared, and open atmosphere inside the corporation is, I believe, more important than the compensation levels of chief executives.

Justifying Unequal Compensation

When salaries are moving upward throughout the corporation, most Americans do not envy those whose achievement and position entail higher salaries than their own; these are what they aspire to achieve themselves. They want a ladder with rungs. Americans resent uniformity. They are performance oriented. For unequal performance, they want unequal pay.

When this general acceptance of understandable inequalities breaks down, sound practice suggests that it is best to look sharply at what is happening in the bottom ranks. Salaries on different levels of an organization should generally rise and fall together. If most people's salaries are going up, practically everybody will be contented. But if salaries at the top keep rising rapidly while those at the bottom fall, stagnate, or rise only slightly, you can be certain feelings of unfairness will arise.

From ancient to modern times, the green worm of envy has been the chief and most regular destroyer of republican experiments: the envy that poisons the innards of one class, section, dynasty, family, or peer against another. Of course, envy never travels under its own name; it is the one vice that never calls itself what it is; it prefers prettier names, good names to which it has no right: "justice," "fairness," and the like. Companies should do everything in their power to defeat envy in every sphere they touch. No vice tears apart democracies more swiftly.

On corporate compensation, therefore, I would make two suggestions. First, one criterion of whether and how annual bonuses should be given—not the only criterion, but an important one—should include consideration of how lower-paid employees are being compensated. At the very least, the direction of compensation levels should be comparable: all should go up, down, or stagnate together, unless clear reasons can be cited for making exceptions in special cases. It may be that in certain crises more is asked of some employees than others, and for this they should be commensurately rewarded, for publicly defended reasons. Also, since half or more of senior executive pay comes by way of bonuses, in years when bonuses are canceled, contractual wages of workers may go up when wages of top executives go down; and that may be fair enough.

Some consideration should also be given to general wage levels outside the corporation. Corporate compensation levels are social facts of great significance in democracies, and they can no longer be hidden. Their public effect must be accounted for in advance. Reasons why they are set where they are set should always be offered to the public, with due forethought given to the public's probable reaction.

Second, for top executives, special new procedures must be designed to protect the neutrality, objectivity, and detachment of those who decide compensation levels, in the full glare of today's communications realities. At present, as the economist Irwin Stelzer has shown,[32] there are too many reasons to suspect lack of sufficient distance between those who serve on compensation committees and those they reward. From an ethical point of view, the real issue is not how much a particular CEO is paid, but by whom, using what methods, according to which criteria, and for what publicly defensible reasons. If an objective case may be made, the social effect is healthy; if the decision reeks of favoritism, the social effect is damaging to the business system as a whole and to democracy.

In such circumstances, envy is certain to uncoil from its slumbers and begin to slither through the body politic. Left-wing politicians feed on envy, but of course do not call it that; they say *compassion*. Envy is distinguished from compassion by a simple test: compassion rejoices in raising up the poor; envy rejoices in pulling down the rich. More than they admit, leftists love to see the rich and powerful humbled.

Against Appeasement

Argument over *governance* is often designed to avoid the main subject: *governors*. Since the point of business is to get things done, argument over governance must not be allowed to suggest the opposite of action—restraint on action or, even worse, process of the sort that pours molasses into the machinery. Reforms of governance must protect sufficient energy in the executive. This freedom to act, in turn, poses new tests for executives in our generation.

Oversight, collective consultation, information gathering, and some division of responsibility—these will always be needed, for reasons rooted in human ignorance, partiality, passion, and fallibility. Intelligent executives, therefore, may well decentralize decision making and rely on decision teams rather than solely on themselves. Their paramount concern is to be in constant touch with reality, and this requires as many eyes and ears, as many dispersed agents of practical wisdom, as possible. But the point of these safeguards is to protect the purposiveness of the corporation. Any scheme of governance that sinks executives in two feet of peanut butter violates the nature of executive institutions: *Executives must be allowed to execute.* They must be helped, strengthened, fully informed, corrected, and reinforced; but, in the end, they must be propelled to step forward to create new wealth.

Furthermore, it is wrong today for executives to conceive of their jobs narrowly, merely in its business aspects, without attention to its political setting and, even more so, to its setting in the world of ideas. Bold in business judgment, executives must not be pusillanimous in politics and mousy in the field of ideas. Let me allude to a recent, and in some ways splendid, report on corporate governance.[33] After reviewing all the powerful voices demanding change in corporate governance, the author, a recently retired CEO, uncharacteristically for him counsels a strategy of appeasement, by way of a preemptive strike. That note of appeasement is the glaring defect in an otherwise excellent analysis.

When reformers demand that corporations become more "responsible," the author rightly notes, they mean *dedicated to causes dear to statists*, such as: executive pay caps, incentives and mandates to cover training and layoffs, constraints on internationalization, demands for a Germanic system of "public interest" corporate directors, and other moves toward the "socialization of corporate America." Before government mandates such things, however, the author argues, businesses should preemptively set out a menu of reforms. His recommendations: broaden stock-option participation to unite the investment interests of workers with those of the corporation, open up paths of decentralized entrepreneurship for employees, and go public against the excessive regulation and unwise social mandates foisted on corporations. These are good suggestions.

Only two things are wrong. First, the author marches them forward under the flag of appeasement: they will punish us less if we punish ourselves first. Second, the former corporate leader magnifies the forces arrayed against corporations in politics and public opinion and fails to summon up the full strength of the intellectual case that corporate leaders can today make to the public.

In the past, preemptive strikes to appease the ferocity of self-assured critics may have been necessary, even the best available response. But in today's very different situation, corporate executives have a new menu of responsibilities. In the economic arena, rather than merely reacting to issues defined by the Left, corporate executives need to set the terms for the national political agenda and to frame public opinion early.

Everyone sees the need for economic growth, even socialists. At their best, however, many executives are still reacting two years too late to issues framed and organized by the Left long before. Much too often, their highest aim is damage limitation. In the arena of public opinion and public policy, tigers in competition have appeared before the public as lambs, bleating in appeasement.

This appeasement has taken two forms: first, intellectual and, second, programs of charitable giving.[34] For some reason, many executives seem defensive about the crucial value of capitalism, business, and corporations to democracy. Knowing that many in the press, the academy, left-wing politics, and political activism are hostile to business and ardent supporters of the party of government, they seem to imagine themselves in a no-win situation; the only question is how much they will lose.

Appeasement seems to them the least harmful solution. Indeed, some critics suggest that people in business secretly feel guilty for becoming wealthy and even enjoy being beaten up in the public eye. I do not believe that, but it is a common theory.

To add insult to injury, these same executives often do, in fact, permit their corporate giving officers to reward with substantial grants the very activists who have advanced legislative agendas aimed at bringing corporate decisions under government control, inch by inch. Such executives no longer sell their enemies the rope by which they will be hanged; they give it to them as a grant.

In the past, such capitulation may have seemed the lesser evil. But now the fading night of the socialist empire, the darkening crisis of the welfare state, and the sepia image of the State as Beneficent Great Provider are yielding to bright Alpine sunlight. Our current intellectual situation is a new spring. Business leaders should study these changes, come abreast of them, and master the new viewpoint they afford.

A Cheerful View at the End of a Sorry Century

The overpromising state of the twentieth century has underachieved, its coffers are bare, and the unintended consequences of its overreaching are disheartening: a pronounced decline in morals and morale, a growing underclass, and a return to serfdom. But look at the contrast: the inventiveness of U.S. corporations and the tough-minded ways in which executives have reshaped them have once again made corporations preeminent.

Today's leading revolutionary force is not the state but the business corporation, turning the mechanical industrial age into the electronic age. Since 1980, corporation-produced miracles such as computers, word processors, fax machines, satellite transmissions, fiber optics, genetic research, and medicines heretofore unseen have transformed the world.

Under Democrats as well as Republicans, the great American job machine has continued to turn out more jobs, and higher-paying jobs, than this country has ever known: more than 50 million new jobs since 1970. Great experiments have also been launched (and already once or twice revised) in corporate structures, management reorganization, work groups, and internal entrepreneurship. Who today can doubt that the most dynamic institution in the world is the business corporation?

Thus, whatever new steps are still to be taken in reforming corporate governance, such steps must protect the inimitable creativity of the business corporation as a unique form of social organization. Its freedom and flexibility are the envy of other institutions. These must be protected, under any and all new schemes for reorganization. If this freedom and flexibility are not protected, the entire society will suffer. In periods of economic decline, the poor suffer most of all.

Only in periods of dynamism and creativity do ever greater numbers of the poor rise out of poverty and discover their own talents for accomplishment. In finding a route out of poverty, second only to small businesses, public corporations are the poor's best friend. That is the main reason why healthy business corporations are the sine qua non for the success of democracy.

Corporate leaders often lose sight of the fact that the most important secondary effect of what they do—not what they aim at, perhaps, but what their actions lead to—is to raise the poor out of poverty and to offer unparalleled opportunities for the development of human talents. Their further great effect is to animate civil society, that huge, bustling arena of the world's grand experiment in self-government. These two signal achievements, raising up the poor and energizing civil society, provide powerful moral claims for business corporations. Corporate leaders should take care that new schemes for corporate governance do not jeopardize these achievements nor distort their one main purpose: to create new wealth for the whole society.

· *Appendix* ·

THE LEGEND OF THE BAY STEED

Once upon a time in Italy, a knight who had been gravely wounded returned home on his sturdy bay warhorse, a beautiful steed whose prancing and snorting, rearing and pawing the air thrilled all the children in the village. Everyone, man and woman alike, admired the beautiful bay. All said that he was the strongest horse they had ever seen. For *Il Re Arturo*—such was his name, an English name, the knight told them, to honor the Knights of the Round Table— not only carried the knight in all his heavy armor with ease; occasionally the brave steed, with the gravely wounded knight's permission, also pulled heavy loads that no other beast in the village could haul.

The wounded knight strictly forbade the townspeople from interfering with the freedom of the horse throughout most of the day. It is important, he said, for the steed to feed quietly and gambol at will around the meadow in which he is fenced.

Later that spring the knight died, and the townspeople inherited the horse and took him under common ownership. They congratulated themselves on all the great tasks they would have *Il Re Arturo* perform for them. One had boulders to remove from his fields. Another had the stumps of two great oaks, partially severed at the roots, to pull free from the earth and drag away. Others had other tasks.

Led by the mayor of the village, in consultation with the priest, the townspeople resolved that each household could use the great bay equally with every other, but whichever household used him that day must feed him that morning and that night. Further, each household must promise to allow him to be free during the height of the day, just as the knight always did, to maintain the steed's spirit and strength.

On the first day, Signor Barone took the steed to move his boulders. He began to feed the horse, but then noting how hot the morning sun already was, decided to hurry him into the field. "He will eat extra tonight," he said. Dragging the boulders took longer than expected, and *Il Re Arturo* got no time to rest—or replenish his spirit—until nearly 4 p.m. At that hour, the horse was bathed in sweat and too fatigued to eat. S. Barone shrugged his shoulders, and said that S. Bucelli would certainly rest the horse on the morrow.

S. Bucelli came early for the horse the next morning, however, and became annoyed because the great steed seemed listless and weary. "It's too early in the day for a great horse like you to be weary," he said. "A little social discipline will straighten you out." He whipped the horse, lightly at first, but more impatiently as the day wore on. After all, the horse was hauling logs to be cut for the village school, an important social project if there ever was one. Thinking that S. Barone must have fed the horse well the night before—"That's probably why he was reluctant to work this morning," Bucelli told himself, "He ate too much," so he fed him only handfuls of oats that night.

On Wednesday, Scarpignato took the horse, and on Thursday, Biaggio; Piccone on Friday; Mastrolilli on Saturday, and on Sunday Padre Umberto rode *Il Re Arturo* over the mountain to say a second Mass at the next village, whose pastor was away visiting his sick mother in another town. Padre Umberto noted that the beautiful horse seemed slow and tired, but he attributed it to the hard climb up the mountain, and the steep descent.

Each day *Il Re Arturo* grew thinner. He was never bathed. No one rubbed down his coat. Each person in the village, knowing how much everybody loved and admired *Il Re Arturo*, assumed that the others were feeding him lavishly. Actually, he was given very little, and never the good grains.

By the end of the summer, *Il Re Arturo* was plainly languishing, grew ill, and died. The village gave him a noble burial. They praised him and all said how much they loved him, and how much he had contributed to the city. Most of their high hopes, of course, now went unfulfilled. They had barely begun the long list of tasks they had first imagined accomplishing. They would accomplish those on the morrow, they said, on some coming lucky morrow, when another gift like *Il Re Arturo* would descend unbidden upon them. They all attributed the good steed's death to grief for his fallen master, the noble knight, whose generosity to the village they vowed never to forget.

They tell the story of the beautiful and powerful horse still today. *Il Re Arturo* grows stronger and more beautiful in every telling.[1]

· *Notes* ·

Introduction

1. Alexis de Tocqueville, *Democracy in America*, ed. J. P. Mayer, trans. G. Lawrence (New York: Doubleday, 1969), pp. 401, 407. All references from Tocqueville in the introduction are drawn from pp. 400–407.

2. Anthony de Jasay, "What's the Big Idea?" *National Review*, July 29, 1996, p. 32.

3. De Jasay notes:

Salvaged from the ruins of socialist thought, the idea that man and society must assert their mastery over the "blind forces of the market" remains central to this "new model." That the bulk of the educated classes is at one with the Left in holding this is not surprising; what is more striking is the strength of this type of discourse on the Right.

Commenting on the sense of entitlement in France, de Jasay continues:

What was unexpected and striking was the clear majority support Bondel and his cohorts got from their victims, the French public, held hostage by the two unions and some public service employees in their fight to protect their perks and privileges. The latter's "acquired" rights were at stake, and true to the medieval spirit in which all have their place and all must keep it, the loss of these rights could not be condoned.

Ibid., pp. 32–35.

4. See Michel Albert, *Capitalisme Contre Capitalisme* (Paris: Le Seuil, 1991). Translated as *Capitalism vs. Capitalism: How America's Obsession with Individual Achievement and Short-Term Profit Has Led It to the Brink of Collapse* (Poplar Falls, Mo.: Four Walls Publishers, 1993). The subtitle seems quaintly out of date.

5. It is not just Europe that differs from America in this regard. As Seymour Martin Lipset has recently observed:

As compared to Australia, Britain, and Europe, Canada is more Whig, less welfare-oriented, and less class-conscious; as contrasted to the United States, it is more group-oriented, more statist, and more communitarian. Robertson Davies, one of Canada's greatest novelists and a Tory, even argues that in spite of Canadians exhibiting a greater "decorum in the discharge of social and political affairs [than Americans] . . . beneath all of this we are a people firmly set in the socialist pattern." The American social structure and values foster the free market and competitive individualism, an orientation which is not congruent with class-consciousness, support for socialist or social democratic parties, or a strong trade union movement.

American Exceptionalism: A Double-Edged Sword (New York: Norton, 1996), p. 108.

6. For 1994, the Bureau of Labor Statistics revealed that "72 percent of the 2.5 million new jobs have been for managers, for professionals . . . and despite its reputation for low wages, the service sector is adding most of the higher wage jobs." Sylvia Nasa, "Statistics Reveal Bulk of New Jobs Pay Over Average," *New York Times*, October 17, 1994, p. A1. Quoted in Lipset, *American Exceptionalism*, p. 57. In the spring of 1996, President Clinton's Council of Economic Advisors found that two-thirds of all new jobs created are in occupations and industries that pay above-average wages. See Karl Zinsmeister, "Indicators," in *The American Enterprise*, July/August 1996, p. 19.

7. See "Venture Capitalists: A Really Big Adventure," *Economist*, January 25, 1997, p. 20.

8. James L. Payne points out that in the early years of Social Security (1945), there were 42 workers paying taxes to support each beneficiary of the program; now there are but 3.3 workers for each beneficiary; in thirty-five years there will be only 2. See his "Security for the Twenty-first Century" in *The American Enterprise*, January/February 1997, pp. 41–44. This entire issue of the magazine features detailed analyses of the Social Security problem.

9. Ben Wattenberg, *The Birth Dearth: What Happens When People in Free Countries Don't Have Enough Babies* (New York: Random House, 1987). Wattenberg notes that between 1957 and 1976, from a higher base, the United States had one of the steepest declines in total fertility rate ever recorded—dropping 54 percent. See pp. 16–17 in particular.

10. See Lipset, *American Exceptionalism*, p. 72. Lipset also shows that only 38 percent of Americans believe the government has a responsibility to reduce income

disparities; the figure is 66 percent in West Germany, 80 percent in Italy (p. 75). For figures on the relative importance of equality and freedom, see Ben Wattenberg, *The First Universal Nation: Leading Indicators and Ideas about the Surge of America in the 1990s* (New York: Free Press, 1991), p. 368.

11. As of 1993, the per capita income of American blacks was $9,806. See *The State of Black America* (Washington, D.C.: National Urban League, 1995), p. 313. For figures on Africa, see *The World Almanac and Book of Facts 1995* (New York: Funk and Wagnalls, 1995), pp. 740–76.

12. "Venture Capitalists," *Economist*, p. 21. Emphasis added.

13. See chapters 1 and 3 of this work. The most recent Federal Reserve data show that 51.3 million Americans own stock directly or through IRAs, mutual funds, or pension plans.

14. "Venture Capitalists," *Economist*, p. 21.

15. See "Financial Aid," editorial, *New York Times*, February 22, 1997, A24.

16. See Abraham Lincoln, "Annual Message to Congress, December 3, 1861," in *Speeches and Writings 1854–1865* (New York: Library of America, 1989), p. 297. Earlier, in a speech at Cincinnati, Ohio, on September 17, 1859, Lincoln offered a moral justification for capital:

That there is a certain relation between capital and labor, I admit. That it does exist, and rightfully exists, I think is true. That men who are industrious, and sober, and honest in the pursuit of their own interests should after a while accumulate capital, and after that should be allowed to enjoy it in peace, and also if they

should choose when they have accumulated it to use it
to save themselves from actual labor and hire other
people to labor for them is right. In doing so they do
not wrong the man they employ, for they find men who
have not of their own land to work upon, or shops to
work in, and who are benefited by working for others,
hired laborers, receiving their capital for it. Thus a few
men that own capital, hire a few others, and these establish the relation of capital and labor rightfully.

Ibid., p. 83.

17. See Oscar Handlin, "The Development of the Corporation," and "The Taxonomy of the Corporation," in *The
Corporation: A Theological Inquiry*, ed. Michael Novak and
John W. Cooper (Washington, D.C.: AEI Press, 1981), pp.
1–33.

18. See the collection edited by F. A. Hayek, *Capitalism
and the Historians* (Chicago: University of Chicago Press,
1954), in particular L. M. Hacker, "The Anticapitalist Bias
of American Historians," pp. 62–90. In his introduction,
Hayek stresses the need for historians to correctly weigh the
impact of capitalism on human emancipation:

[T]here is no reason why we should not respect the motives of some of those who, to arouse public conscience,
painted the misery of the poor in the blackest colors.
We owe to agitation of this kind, which forced unwill-
ing eyes to face unpleasant facts, some of the finest and
most generous acts of public policy—from the aboli-
tion of slavery to the removal of taxes on imported food
and the destruction of many entrenched monopolies
and abuses. And there is every reason to remember

how miserable the majority of the people still were as recently as a hundred or a hundred and fifty years ago. But we must not, long after the event, allow a distortion of the facts, even if committed out of humanitarian zeal, to affect our view of what we owe to a system which for the first time in history made people feel that this misery might be avoidable. The very claims and ambitions of the working classes were and are the result of the enormous improvement of their position which capitalism brought about. There were, no doubt, many people whose privileged position, whose power to secure a comfortable income by preventing others from doing better what they were being paid for, was destroyed by the advance of freedom of enterprise. There may be various other grounds on which the development of modern industrialism might be deplored by some; certain aesthetic and moral values to which the privileged upper classes attached great importance were no doubt endangered by it. Some people might even question whether the rapid increase of population, or, in other words, the decrease in infant mortality, was a blessing. But if, and in so far as, one takes as one's test the effect on the standard of life of the large number of the toiling classes, there can be little doubt that this effect was to produce a general upward trend. (pp. 25–26)

Forty years on, the problem Hayek is addressing in this passage is still with us: witness the best-selling book of William Greider, *One World, Ready or Not: The Manic Logic of Global Capitalism* (New York: Simon & Schuster, 1996). While Greider admits that "Economic revolution . . .

liberates masses of people," it also "projects new aspects of tyranny":

> Masses of people are also tangibly deprived of their claims to self-sufficiency, the independent means of sustaining hearth and home. People and communities, even nations, find themselves losing control over their own destinies, ensnared by the revolutionary demands of commerce.
>
> The great paradox of this economic revolution is that its new technologies enable people and nations to take sudden leaps into modernity, while at the same time they promote the renewal of once-forbidden barbarisms. Amid the newness of things, exploitation of the weak by the strong also flourishes again.
>
> The present economic revolution, like revolutions of the past, is fueled by invention and human ingenuity and a universal aspiration to build and accumulate. But it is also driven by a palpable sense of insecurity. No one can be said to control the energies of unfettered capital, not important governments or financiers, not dictators or democrats.
>
> And, in the race to the future, no one dares to fall a step behind, not nations or major corporations. Even the most effective leaders of business and finance share in the uncertainty, knowing as they do that the uncompromising dynamics can someday turn on the revolutionaries themselves. (p. 12)

19. Michael Novak, *The Spirit of Democratic Capitalism* (Lanham, Md.: Madison Books, 1982, 1991).

20. *Toward a Theology of the Corporation*, rev. ed. (Washington, D.C.: AEI Press, 1990).

21. Michael Novak, *Business as a Calling: Work and the Examined Life* (New York: Free Press, 1996).

Chapter 1

1. As the doyen of American socialist historians wrote in 1990, "Less than seventy-five years after it officially began, the contest between capitalism and socialism is over: capitalism has won." Robert Heilbroner, "Was the Right Right All Along?" *Harper's*, January 1991, p. 18.

2. Early on, Hutton indicates the thinkers in the American tradition whom he considers allies: John Kenneth Galbraith, Robert Reich, and Lester Thurow. See Will Hutton, *The State We're In* (London: Jonathan Cape, 1995), p. xi.

3. *Newsweek*, February 26, 1996, pp. 44–51.

4. Alan MacFarlane, *The Culture of Capitalism* (London: Blackwell, 1987), p. 189.

5. All but approximately 44,000 of these firms employ fewer than 20 persons. All figures in this and the next paragraph are from *Statistical Abstract of the United States 1995* (Washington, D.C.: U.S. Department of Commerce, 1996).

6. An important note: Since in many cities great new hospital facilities, with their attendant research institutes, are now the single largest employer, and since some state universities have more employees than even the largest business corporations in their states, the number and type of entities covered by the terms *corporate law*, *corporate governance*, and even *business corporation* are quite vast. Not all hospital complexes these days, for example, are nonprofits. But even the so-called nonprofits actually need to

budget each year for future improvements and new technologies and therefore must operate with an annual excess of income over existing costs; this is very like a profit margin. And in not a few of their activities these days, universities are divided into what are, in effect, profit centers.

7. Paul Johnson further states, "The transformation took place when the Benedictine or Benedictine-type rule was grafted on to earlier forms. Thus the foundation at Fontanelle on the banks of the lower Seine, near Rouen . . . became a major agricultural colony after adopting a regular discipline in the mid-seventh century." Paul Johnson, *A History of Christianity* (New York: Atheneum, 1980), pp. 148–49.

8. See Luigi Sturzo, *Church and State*, vol. I (Notre Dame: University of Notre Dame Press, 1962), pp. 36–37. Another account is given by Newman C. Eberhardt, C.M., *A Summary of Catholic History, Vol. I: Ancient and Medieval History* (St. Louis: B. Herder Book Co., 1961), pp. 163–64.

9. Friedrich A. Hayek, *New Studies in Philosophy, Politics and Economics* (London: Routledge & Kegan Paul, 1978), p. 260.

10. Kazua Noda, "The Corporation," *The New Encyclopaedia Britannica*, Macropaedia, 5 (Chicago: H.H. Benton, 1977), p. 183.

11. In the first of his 1959 Wabash lectures on economics and freedom, the historian Jacob Viner noted: "It was a commonplace of Greek and Roman thought, destined to be absorbed in the Christian tradition, that trade was either by its inherent nature, or through the temptations it offered to those engaged in it, pervasively associated with fraud and cheating, especially, according to Cicero, if it were 'small,' or retail trade." Jacob Viner, *Essays on the Intellectual*

History of Economics, ed. D. Irwin (Princeton: Princeton University Press, 1991), p. 39.

12. See my *Business as a Calling* (New York: Free Press, 1996).

13. Oscar Handlin, "The Development of the Corporation," in *The Corporation: A Theological Inquiry*, ed. M. Novak and J. Cooper (Washington, D.C.: AEI Press, 1981), p. 10.

14. Ibid., p. 10: "They were not all going somewhere. But some of them were; and they permitted the penetration of areas even before the passengers and the freight they would carry appeared. In the same way, a whole series of new economic opportunities were able to be exploited at the end of the century because the device of the corporation permitted the rapid mobilization of large amounts of capital, of managerial ability, and of the enterprise to bring these processes to a successful conclusion."

15. Ibid., p. 2.

16. Oakeshott defined the "enterprise association" as a "relationship in terms of the pursuit of some common purpose, some substantive condition of things to be jointly procured, or some common interest to be continuously satisfied." This was to distinguish it from a "civil association," rule-governed but not focused on particular ends. See Michael Oakeshott, *On Human Conduct* (Oxford: Oxford University Press, 1975), p. 114.

17. Peter Drucker, *The Concept of the Corporation* (New York: The John Day Co., 1946), pp. 20–21.

18. Tocqueville wrote:

While the law allows the American people to do everything, there are things which religion prevents them

from imagining and forbids them to dare. Religion, which never intervenes directly in the government of American society, should therefore be considered as the first of their political institutions, for although it did not give them the taste of liberty, it singularly facilitates their use thereof.

Alexis de Tocqueville, *Democracy in America*, ed. J.P. Mayer, trans. G. Lawrence (New York: Anchor Books, 1966), p. 292.

19. In Hamilton's words:

It has been frequently remarked that it seems to have been reserved to the people of this country, by their conduct and example, to decide the important question, whether societies of men are really capable or not of establishing good government from *reflection* and *choice* or whether they are forever destined to depend for their political constitutions on accident and force. [Emphasis added.]

Alexander Hamilton, James Madison, and John Jay, *The Federalist Papers*, intro. by C. Rossiter (New York: New American Library, 1961), p. 33.

20. The phrase "commercial republic" was first developed by Montesquieu, in trying to understand why England, the nation of shopkeepers and property owners, seemed in all Europe to be so well governed and her manners so agreeable. The concept was well argued over by the founders, as in *Federalist* No. 6, and formed the backbone of the tradition called "commercial republicanism" and "civic republicanism" here and "civic humanism" by

Adam Smith in Scotland. See Ralph Lerner, "Commerce and Character: The Anglo-American as New-Model Man," in Ralph Lerner, *The Thinking Revolutionary: Principle and Practice in the New Republic* (Ithaca, N.Y.: Cornell University Press, 1987), pp. 185–221; see also John Robertson, "Adam Smith as Civic Moralist," in *Wealth and Virtue: The Shaping of Political Economy in the Scottish Enlightenment*, ed. Istvan Hont and Michael Ignatieff (Cambridge: Cambridge University Press, 1983), pp. 179–202.

21. See Baron de Montesquieu, *The Spirit of the Laws*, translated by T. Nugent (New York: Macmillan, 1949), Book xx, chaps. 1, 2, 7, 8.

22. Jerry Ellis, Joint Economic Committee, 104th U.S. Congress, "We Have Met the Corporations and They Us," unpublished working paper proposed for the JEC, 104th Congress, 1996.

23. See William Safire's "On Language," *New York Times Magazine*, May 5, 1996, pp. 26–27.

24. See Giovanni Sartori, "The Market, Planning, Capitalism and Democracy," *This World*, vol. 5 (Spring/Summer 1983), pp. 68–71.

25. Tocqueville, *Democracy in America*, pp. 691–92.

26. Hutton, *The State We're In*, chap. 9.

27. Hayek outlined his proposal for the privatization of money in *The Denationalization of Money* (London: Institute of Economic Affairs, 1978).

28. Hutton writes:

There are . . . no legal requirements for audit committees to provide alternative sources of financial information to the nonexecutive directors. There are no

independent remuneration committees to assess directors' pay. There is no system for ensuring that the cus-
todians of company pension funds are independent.
Firms do not have to establish supervisory boards to
monitor the performance of their executive board as
they do in Europe; rather the board is judge and jury of
its own performance. There is no formal incorporation
of key stakeholders—trade unions and banks—in the
constitution of the firm. There is no obligation to establish works councils or to recognise trade unions as partners in the enterprise. The public cannot easily obtain
company information. Transparent and commonly accepted accounting guidelines are not enforced, and can
vary hugely from firm to firm or from year to year; the
annual report and accounts set out precisely what the
board and its chairman decide they will set out. The
firm is a law unto itself, sovereign of all it surveys. Its
only job is to succeed in the marketplace.

Hutton, *The State We're In*, p. 295.

29. One may speak of "sovereignty of the self" when one
means self-government with reference to other human beings—the sense in which citizens of the United States are
"sovereign citizens," able to act as "We the People" in
erecting a government based on their consent. Face to face
with God, the governor of our autonomy, we are subjects,
not sovereigns. This is the sense in which we say that it is
the truth that makes us free; "And ye shall know the truth,
and the truth shall make you free" (John 8:32).

30. Ralph Estes, "Antidote to Economic Anxiety,"
Washington Post, May 19, 1996.

31. Reich, in a February 6, 1996, speech at George

Washington University, "Pinkslips, Profits, and Paychecks: Corporate Citizenship in an Era of Smaller Government," emphasized the "narrow economic calculus" that motivates corporations and proposed the following:

> If we want companies to do things which do not necessarily improve the returns to shareholders but which are beneficial for the economy and society as a whole . . . we have to give business an economic reason to do so. One possibility would be to reduce or eliminate corporate income taxes only for companies that achieve certain minimum requirements along these dimensions.

Quoted in Joint Economic Committee, 104th U.S. Congress, "Corporate Responsibility or Company Store? Secretary Reich's Regressive Proposal," February 1996.

Chapter 2

1. Abraham Lincoln, "Lecture on Discoveries and Inventions," Jacksonville, Illinois, February 11, 1859, in *Speeches and Writings: 1859–1865* (Washington, D.C.: Library of America, 1989), p. 4.

2. It is interesting that Lincoln emphasizes the role of social habit in the dynamic of economic growth. For two recent works that empirically explore the role of such habits in economic success, see Francis Fukuyama, *Trust: The Social Virtues and the Creation of Prosperity* (New York: Free Press, 1995), pp. 43–48; and Thomas Sowell, *Migrations*

and Cultures: A World View (New York: Basic Books, 1996), pp. 371–91.

3. The constitutional scholar Robert Goldwin underscores Lincoln's point:

> Lincoln made a helpful distinction. Genius has its own fire. The desire to decipher the mysteries of nature and of nature's laws, to make something that has never before existed, to say what has never before been said— these have a compelling power of their own. The love of wisdom or knowledge or understanding is, in a significant way, nonpolitical, nonsocietal. Its motivation is internal. It cannot be originated by constitutional provisions, no matter how skillfully drawn and implemented. But it can be fueled—encouraged, nurtured, protected, rewarded, and thus enhanced.
>
> Genius, the power and originality of mind that produces new thought, new understanding, new inventions, has its own "fire" that society at-large cannot plan, schedule, or produce. It ignites, happily, in unpredictable persons, times, and places, and when it does it is an individual and private matter.
>
> But societies need such innovative genius; they neglect it at the risk of their own impoverishment. What the framers understood, and what Lincoln's sentence illuminates so well, is that the best that society at-large can do is provide more fuel for the fire of genius.

Why Blacks, Women, and Jews Are Not Mentioned in the Constitution, and Other Unorthodox Views (Washington, D.C.: AEI Press, 1990), p. 40.

4. See Fred Warshofsky, *The Patent Wars: The Battle*

to Own the World's Technology (New York: John Wiley & Sons, Inc., 1994), p. 8.

5. See Thomas Jefferson, "A Summary View of the Rights of British America," in Thomas Jefferson, *Writings* (Washington, D.C.: Library of America, 1984), p. 122.

6. The pope adds:

The modern *business economy* has positive aspects. Its basis is human freedom exercised in the economic field, just as it is exercised in many other fields . . . and like every other sector, it includes the right to freedom, as well as the duty of making responsible use of freedom.

Pope John Paul II, *Centesimus Annus* (Washington, D.C.: United States Catholic Conference, 1991), no. 32. For an extended treatment of this encyclical, see my *Catholic Ethic and the Spirit of Capitalism* (New York: Free Press, 1993), pp. 114–43; and Richard John Neuhaus, *Doing Well and Doing Good* (New York: Doubleday, 1992).

7. *Centesimus Annus*, no. 32.

8. There are now more than 1 billion Catholics, more than half in the third world. Note also the *political* contributions of the American experiment to the thought of Pope John Paul II:

Pope Leo XIII was aware of the need for a sound *theory of the State* in order to ensure the normal development of man's spiritual and temporal activities, both of which are indispensable. For this reason, in one passage of *Rerum Novarum* [1891] he presents the organization of society according to the three powers—legislative, executive and judicial—, something which at the time represented a novelty in Church teaching. Such an ordering reflects a realistic vision of man's social nature, which calls for legislation capable of protecting the freedom of all. To that end, it is preferable that each power be balanced by other powers and by other spheres of responsibility which keep it within proper bounds. This is the principle of the "rule of law," in which the law is sovereign, and not the arbitrary will of individuals. [Ibid., no. 44]

See Russell Hittinger, "The Pope and the Liberal State," *First Things* (December 1992), pp. 33–41.

9. Warshofsky, *Patent Wars*, p. 3.

10. For the history of these events, consult Karl Fenning, "The Origin of the Patent and Copyright Clause of the Constitution," *Georgetown Law Journal*, 1921, pp. 109–17. For the earlier history of patent and copyright law, see Paul Goldstein, *Copyright's Highway: The Law and Lore of Copyright from Gutenberg to the Celestial Jukebox* (New York: Hill and Wang, 1994), pp. 37–77. The first international agreements on patents and copyrights did not occur until much later—the Paris Convention of 1883 and the Berne Convention of 1886. For more on the history of these laws, see William P. Kingston, *The Political Economy of Innovation* (The Hague: Martinus Nijhuff Publishers, 1984), pp. 100–104. See also Arthur R. Miller and Michael H. Davis, *Intellectual Property: Patents, Trademarks and Copyright* (St. Paul, Minn.: West Publishing Co., 1983), esp. chaps. 1 and 10.

11. Concerning patents and copyrights, James Madison writes in *The Federalist Papers* No. 43 (New York: New American Library, 1961):

The utility of this power will scarcely be questioned. The copyright of authors has been solemnly adjudged in Great Britain to be a right at Common Law. The right to useful inventions seems with equal reason to belong to the inventors. The public good fully coincides in both cases with the claims of individuals. [pp. 271–72]

12. See Goldstein, *Copyright's Highway*, pp. 9–10.

13. See "Are Patents and Copyrights Morally Justified? The Philosophy of Property Rights and Ideal Objects," *Harvard Journal of Law and Public Policy*, vol. 13 (1989), pp. 817–65. As Palmer puts it, "Intellectual property rights are rights in ideal objects, which are distinguished from the material substrata in which they are instantiated," p. 818.

14. Wendy J. Gordon, "An Inquiry into the Merits of Copyright: The Challenges of Consistency, Consent, and Encouragement Theory," *Stanford Law Review*, vol. 41 (1989), pp. 1365–1477.

15. See Palmer, "Are Patents and Copyrights Morally Justified?" (p. 829), quoting William Leggett, the nineteenth-century Jacksonian editorialist: "If you assert an exclusive right to a particular idea, you cannot be sure that the very same idea did not at the same moment enter some other mind." Palmer calls this the "problem of simultaneous invention or discovery."

16. Gordon, "An Inquiry into the Merits of Copyright," p. 1369.

17. See also Lincoln's "Address to the Wisconsin State Agricultural Society" (also of 1859), where he pays eloquent homage to the role invention plays in agriculture:

I know of nothing so pleasant to the mind, as the discovery of anything which is at once *new* and *valuable*—nothing which so lightens and sweetens toil, as the hopeful pursuit of such discovery. And how vast, and how varied a field is agriculture, for such discovery. The mind, already trained to thought, in the country school, or higher school, cannot fail to find there an exhaustless source of profitable enjoyment. Every blade of grass is a study; and to produce two, where there was but one, is both a profit and a pleasure. And not grass alone; but soils, seeds, and seasons—hedges, ditches, and fences, draining, droughts, and irrigation—plowing, hoeing, and harrowing—reaping, mowing, and threshing—saving crops, pests of crops, diseases of crops, and what will prevent or cure them— implements, utensils, and machines, their relative merits, and how to improve them—hogs, horses, and cattle—sheep, goats, and poultry—trees, shrubs, fruits, plants, and flowers—the thousand things of which these are specimens—each a world of study within itself.

Speeches and Writings: 1859–1865, pp. 99–100.

18. Robert P. Benko, *Protecting Intellectual Property Rights: Issues and Controversies* (Washington, D.C.: American Enterprise Institute, 1987).

19. As in the utilitarian tradition. See Palmer, "Are Patents and Copyrights Morally Justified?" pp. 820, 849–51.

20. Gordon mentions the philosopher Alan Ryan in this regard. See Gordon, "An Inquiry into the Merits of Copyrights," p. 1345. For Ryan, see *The Political Theory of Property* (Oxford: Blackwell, 1984), pp. 163–64. For the

ur-text of this left-wing term, see C. B. Macpherson, *The Political Theory of Possessive Individualism* (Oxford: Clarendon Press, 1962). Many who affect to despise the concept practice it.

21. As my AEI colleague Christopher DeMuth has emphasized to me, it is a confusion to call patents and copyrights "monopolies," because monopoly depends on conditions of market supply and demand: a monopoly is a good supplied by a single supplier *that has no close substitutes in use*. Thus, a patent or copyright *may* confer monopoly pricing power—but so may a property right in something tangible, such as a strategically located parcel of land. Moreover, a patent or copyright confers no monopoly where there are satisfactory substitutes for the new invention or writing. In other words, both "intellectual" and "tangible" property rights may lead to monopoly, but the purpose (and general effect) of those rights is to promote rather than to restrict competition and economic output.

22. See Palmer, "Are Patents and Copyrights Morally Justified?" pp. 860–61.

23. In his recent book, *The Heroic Enterprise*, John Hood tells the story of Dr. Raymond Damadian, the inventor of the magnetic resonance imaging (MRI) device, one of the most important medical advances of the past few decades whose primary use is to find cancers that otherwise might go undiagnosed for years:

Damadian began working on the idea in 1970 and, with a colleague, began testing the technology on rats at a private research lab in Pittsburgh. Proving the concept to be workable, Damadian obtained a patent in 1974 and by 1977 had tested an MRI scanner on a human being. The following year, Damadian and his coworkers started FONAR Corporation to manufacture MRI scanners. By 1982 large domestic and foreign companies decided the concept made sense and began introducing their own MRI products despite Damadian's patent. Over the next few years, even as FONAR pursued legal action, the company continued to refine MRI technology, generating more than 80 percent of all the innovations in the industry and securing another twenty patents. But every innovation the company introduced was promptly copied by its largest competitors. . . . Even though patents protect innovative companies from having their ideas stolen by others, they do not protect these firms from competition. In virtually every case where a drug has been introduced to treat a medical condition, alternative treatments for that condition exist, sometimes including other patented drugs.

The Heroic Enterprise: Business and the Common Good (New York: Free Press, 1996), p. 100.

24. See Goldstein, *Copyright's Highway*, chaps. 4 and 6, for the complexity of the new problems.

25. See Philip E. Ross, "Cops versus Robbers in Cyberspace," *Forbes*, September 9, 1996, pp. 134–39. See also Goldstein, *Copyright's Highway*, pp. 158–64, on the history behind the Audio Home Recording Act of 1992. Wendy J. Gordon notes an important psychological difference that often attends theft of intellectual property:

One need climb no fences to make copies of intellectual products. . . . One knows one is doing something wrong when one tries to sneak into a neighbor's house or pick the lock of another's automobile; it may not seem so obviously wrong to tape a musical recording or duplicate a computer program that is already in hand. In addition, an act of copying seems to harm no one. There is no perceptible loss, no shattered lock or broken fencepost, no blood, not even a psychological sense of trespass.

Gordon, "An Inquiry into the Merits of Copyright," p. 1346.

26. See Andrew Kimbrell, "Patents Encroach upon the Body," *Crisis*, May 1993, pp. 43–48. Kimbrell's book, *The Human Body Shop* (San Francisco: HarperCollins, 1993), develops his argument at length.

27. See Wilson's book, *The Moral Sense* (New York: Free Press, 1993) for his full treatment of the moral sentiments, an emphasis given prominence by the Scottish Enlightenment.

28. Pope John Paul II, "Address to Pontifical Academy of Sciences," *L'Osservatore Romano*, November 1994, p. 3.

29. The argument on the moral status of biogenetic experimentation and gene patenting is well under way. In May of 1996, for example, the American Enterprise Institute held a day-long conference, "The Ethics of Gene Patenting." For Richard D. Land and C. Ben Mitchell, see "Patenting Life: No," *First Things*, May 1996, pp. 20–22. In the same issue, Ted Peters weighs in on the other side with "Patenting Life: Yes," pp. 18–19. Both arguments were responding to a May 18, 1995, press conference held by a group of religious leaders in Washington, D.C. The conference called for a ban on patenting human genes and

genetically engineered animals. Led by the naturalist Jeremy Rifkin, those endorsing the "Joint Appeal against Human and Animal Patenting" included Rabbi Saperstein (director of the Religious Action Center of Reform Judaism); Abdurahman Alamoudi (executive director of the American Muslim Council); and Wesley Granberg Michaelson (secretary general of the Reformed Church in America). Rifkin summed up the appeal: "By turning life into patented inventions, the government drains life of its intrinsic nature and sacred value." For an extremely clear presentation of the case for the moral legitimacy of gene patents, see Baruch A. Brody, "On Patenting Transgenic Animals," *The Ag Bioethics Forum*, vol. 7, no. 2 (November 1995). Brody argues that opposition to gene patenting tends to invest nature with a sacredness at odds with Jewish and Christian teaching on man's dominion over nature.

30. Land and Mitchell do not object in their article in *First Things* to the creation of such creatures as the "oncomouse"—a mouse genetically engineered to carry a cancer gene useful for human cancer research—but do object to patenting it: "While animal ownership per se is morally acceptable, patenting animals represents an abuse of the notion of ownership, and more importantly of ownership rights." Land and Mitchell, "Patenting Life: No," p. 20. Elsewhere, however, Land seemingly rejects the genetic engineering itself by describing "altering life forms, creating new life forms, as a revolt against the sovereignty of God and an attempt to be God." Quoted in Peters, "Patenting Life: Yes," p. 19. What often disguises itself as an antipatenting position is in reality a profound distrust of man's prometheanism.

31. Although Land and Mitchell admit that "whole

human beings have not been patented," they are troubled by the fact that "by September 4, 1993, the National Institutes of Health had filed for patents on 6,122 gene fragments. Although patenting of 'gene fragments of unknown biological function' is presently disallowed, who knows what the future holds?" Land and Mitchell, "Patenting Life: No," p. 20.

32. On embryo cloning, the Italian philosopher Rocco Buttiglione writes:

> The real issue is not embryo cloning; the issue has to do with love, responsibility and family. Only in this way can the child establish close ties—that mix of love and authority that is moral education—which will enable him to become a mature, responsible individual in a free society. That kind of person cannot be "produced" in a laboratory. If we try to "produce" a child as if he were a machine, or a commodity on an assembly line, we do not respect his dignity.

"Immoral Clones: A Vatican View," *New Perspectives Quarterly*, vol. 3, no. 1 (Winter 1994).

33. See "Advance Reported on Sickle Cell Anemia," *New York Times*, September 6, 1996.

34. Pope John Paul II, "Address to Pontifical Academy of Sciences," p. 3.

35. Walter Lippmann calls this the "public philosophy." See his book, *The Public Philosophy* (Rutgers, N.J.: Transaction Publishers, 1989). See also the work of Jacques Maritain, in particular, *The Degrees of Knowledge*, ed. R. McInerny, trans. G. Phelan (Notre Dame, Ind.: University of Notre Dame Press, 1996).

36. Bernard Lonergan, *Insight: A Study of Human Understanding* (New York: Longmans, 1957), p. 4.

37. Friedrich von Hayek, *The Fatal Conceit: The Errors of Socialism*, ed. W. W. Bartley III (Chicago: University of Chicago Press, 1989), pp. 36–37.

38. This is why I find it difficult to understand this passage from Pope John Paul II's "Address to Pontifical Academy of Sciences":

> On this subject, we rejoice that numerous researchers have refused to allow discoveries made about the genome to be patented. Since the human body is not an object that can be disposed of at will, the results of research should be made available to the whole scientific community and cannot be the property of a small group. [p. 3]

It is only fair to note that Hayek and the pope agree on this point. So far as I can discover, however, the Vatican has not otherwise addressed the general role of patents in serving the common good.

39. Hayek, *The Fatal Conceit*, p. 22.

40. See Peter Huber, "Private Property," a review of James Boyle, *Shamans, Software and Spleens*, in *New York Times Book Review*, September 22, 1996, p. 18.

41. Edmund W. Kitch, "The Nature and Function of the Patent System," *Journal of Law and Economics*, vol. 20 (October 1977), pp. 265–90.

42. Take, for example, the pharmaceutical industry, where 18.8 percent of sales is devoted to "R&D" and where the odds of developing a useful new drug from original conception to marketplace delivery are 1 in 5,000. The process

requires an average investment of $450 million, fifty disci-
plines, and twelve to fifteen years of work. See "Protecting
Intellectual Property in the Pharmaceutical Industry—A
Critical Key to Worldwide Health and Economic Development" (unpublished manuscript, Pfizer, 1996); see also
chap. 6 of Hood, *The Heroic Enterprise*, pp. 96–129.

43. Quoted in Huber, "Private Property," p. 18.

44. For a perhaps surprising recognition of the benefits
of investment by multinational corporations for developing
nations, see John Kenneth Galbraith, "The Defense of
the Multinational Company," *Harvard Business Review*
(March–April 1979), pp. 83–93. See more recently, Irwin
M. Stelzer, "Nice Town, Shantytown," *Weekly Standard*,
September 16, 1996, pp. 18–20. See also chap. 8 of my
book *Business as a Calling: Work and the Examined Life*
(New York: Free Press, 1996), pp. 160–75. On the role of
patent protection in the developing world, see Edmund W.
Kitch, "The Patent Policy of Developing Countries," *UCLA
Pacific Basin Law Journal*, vol. 13, 1994, pp. 166–78.

45. As Aristotle put it:

> Moral excellence is concerned with pleasure and pains;
> it is on account of the pleasure that we do bad things,
> and on account of the pain that we abstain from noble
> ones. Hence we ought to have been brought up in a
> particular way from our very youth . . . so as both to
> delight in and to be pained by the things we ought; for
> this is the right education.

Nicomachean Ethics, trans. W. D. Ross, book II, chap. 3 in
The Basic Works of Aristotle, ed. Richard McKeon (New
York: Random House, 1941), p. 954.

Chapter 3

1. The most influential is, as discussed in chapter 1, Britain's Will Hutton, with his elastic concept of "stakeholding" (see also note 12, below). A moderate statement among recent studies is *Ownership and Control: Rethinking Corporate Governance for the Twenty-first Century*, Margaret W. Blair (Washington, D.C.: Brookings Institution, 1995); more critical and deeper is *The Genius of American Corporate Law*, Roberta Romano (Washington, D.C.: AEI Press, 1993); a study by two leaders in the stakeholder movement is Robert A. G. Marks and Nell Minow, *Watching the Watchers: Corporate Governance for the 21st Century* (Cambridge, Mass.: Blackwell, 1996).

2. Adam Smith, *An Inquiry into the Nature and Causes of the Wealth of Nations*, vol. II, ed. R. H. Campbell and A. S. Skinner (Indianapolis, Ind.: Liberty Classics, 1981), p. 741.

3. As Karl Marx and Friedrich Engels wrote: "The bourgeoisie, during its rule of scarce one hundred years, has created more massive and more colossal productive forces than have all preceding generations together. Subjection of Nature's forces to man, machinery, application of chemistry to industry and agriculture, steam-navigation, railways, electric telegraphs, clearing of whole continents for cultivation, canalization of rivers, whole populations conjured out of the ground—what earlier century had even a presentiment that such productive forces slumbered in the lap of social labor?" *The Communist Manifesto* (New York: International Publishers, 1948), pp. 13–14.

4. Of Japanese corporate life, Peter Drucker has written: "In Japan . . . the large employer—government agency

or business—has increasingly attempted to become a 'community' for its employees. 'Lifetime employment' is only one affirmation of this. Company housing, company health plans, company vacations, and so on, all emphasize for the Japanese employee that the employer, and especially the big corporation, is the community and the successor to yesterday's family."

But Drucker himself has noted the shift in Japan away from this idea in recent years, a result of the growing number of people who earn their living through brain-power: "The young knowledge people in Japan still sing the company song. They still expect the company to provide them job security. However, not only do they refuse, increasingly, to sacrifice their family life to the company, but they increasingly are as ready as their counterparts to change jobs if there is a better one available." *Managing in a Time of Great Change* (New York: Dutton, 1995), pp. 253–54.

Francis Fukuyama has also recently explored the changing corporate culture of Japan in his *Trust: The Social Virtues and the Creation of Prosperity* (New York: Free Press, 1995), pp. 161–93. See also Jonathan P. Charkham, "Japan," in *Keeping Good Company: A Study of Corporate Governance in Five Countries* (Oxford: Clarendon Press, 1994), pp. 70–118, esp. p. 71.

5. See Michael Oakeshott, *On Human Conduct* (Oxford: Oxford University Press, 1975). To repeat: Oakeshott defines an enterprise association as "substantive; it is an association in cooperative 'doing.' And there may be as many such associations as there are purposes to invoke joint pursuit" (p. 315). A civil association, in contrast, is "formal; not in terms of the satisfaction of substantive wants but in terms of the conditions to be observed in seeking the

satisfaction of wants" (p. 313). (For Oakeshott, government must be viewed as a civic association, that is, "formal" and "rule governed"; otherwise, it would be led to impose substantive ways of acting and being on free persons, thus denying their liberty.)

6. Irving Kristol led me to this insight: "You can't have 'separation of powers' within corporate leadership any more than you can have separation of powers within the executive branch of government." "What Is a CEO Worth?" *Wall Street Journal*, June 5, 1996.

7. As Alexander Hamilton wrote in *The Federalist Papers* No. 70 (New York: New American Library, 1961): "Energy in the executive is the leading character in the definition of good government. It is essential to the protection of the community against foreign attacks; it is not less essential to the steady administration of the laws; to the protection of property against those irregular and high-handed combinations which sometimes interrupt the ordinary cause of justice; to the security of liberty against the enterprises and assaults of ambition, of faction, and of anarchy" (p. 423).

8. See my *Choosing Our King: Powerful Symbols in Presidential Politics* (New York: Macmillan, 1974), recently reissued and expanded as *Choosing Presidents: Symbols of Political Leadership* (Rutgers, N.J.: Transaction, 1992), esp. part one, "Priest, Prophet, King," pp. 3–53.

9. On the functions of boards, see William G. Bowen, *Inside the Boardroom: Governance by Directors and Trustees* (New York: John Wiley & Sons, Inc., 1944), pp. 17–38. His list includes these: to select, encourage, and if necessary replace CEOs; to adopt long-term strategy; to ensure resources will match the strategy; to monitor management; and to nominate strong candidates for the board.

Persons with experience on corporate boards have stressed to me that boards have two chief general functions, which need to be finely balanced: first, to give counsel about upcoming decisions; second, to monitor ongoing structures, practices, and actions. Too much of one, to the neglect of the other, is a bad mistake. Respecting these two tendencies, the ideal board should be balanced, even temperamentally.

10. As Aristotle wrote, "Precision is not to be sought for alike in all discussions, any more than in all the products of the crafts . . . it is the mark of an educated man to look for precision in each class of things just so far as the nature of the subject admits." *Nicomachean Ethics*, trans. W. D. Ross, book I, chap. 2, in *The Basic Works of Aristotle*, ed. R. McKeon (New York: Random House, 1941), p. 936.

11. See, for example, Drucker's *The Concept of the Corporation* (New York: Harper & Row Library, 1946), chap. 2; and *Managing in a Time of Great Change*: "With the emergence of the knowledge society, society has become a society of organizations. Most of us work in and for an organization, are dependent for our effectiveness and equally for our living on access to an organization, whether as an organization's employee or as provider of services to an organization—as a lawyer, for instance, or a freight forwarder. And more and more of these supporting services to organizations are, themselves, organized as organizations. The first law firm was organized in the United States a little over a century ago—until then lawyers practiced as individuals. In Europe there were no law firms to speak of until after World War II. Today, the practice of law is increasingly done in larger and larger partnerships. But that is also true, especially in the United States, of the practice of medicine. The knowledge society is a society of organizations in

which practically every single social task is being performed in and through an organization" (p. 245).

12. As in Will Hutton's influential *The State We're In* (London: Vintage, 1996), which has had an effect on Tony Blair's vision of transforming England into a "stakeholder" society. For a powerful critique of Hutton and other advocates of Britain's New Labour, see David Willetts, *Blair's Gurus* (London: Centre for Policy Studies, 1996), esp. pp. 13–24. See also chapter 1, "The Future of the Corporation," of this volume.

13. See David Brock's discussion of Hillary Rodham Clinton's path to statism, in *The Seduction of Hillary Rodham* (New York: Free Press, 1996), pp. 112–16.

14. It is a serious error, for example, for IBM to bow to the demands of activists and extend their health plans to pay for domestic partners of homosexual relationships. Domestic partners are not spouses; acts of sodomy—the distinguishing feature of gay relationships—are not morally equivalent to marital acts; and ceding such moral equivalence is a serious moral step not submitted to shareholders for their approval. IBM, in fact, extends spousal benefits *only* to homosexual couples, refusing to do so in the case of heterosexual couples living together without being married. Nationwide, 313 companies, including Disney and Coors, have embraced spousal benefits for homosexual couples. See Norman Podhoretz, "How the Gay Rights Movement Won," *Commentary* (November 1996), pp. 32–41.

15. Witness the role played by certain corporations in the struggle against the 1996 CCRI, a ballot initiative that will end state-sponsored race and gender preferences throughout California. As Heather Mac Donald writes: "The lovefest between the advocates and the corporate

establishment depends partly on corporate self-interest. Businesses pay off the anti-discrimination machine in the hope of inoculating themselves against litigation. But the relationship has another basis as well: There exists inside corporations a parallel network of activists who share the same goals as, and maintain close contact with, the civil rights groups. This is the internal affirmative action appa-ratus, a fearsome bureaucracy that just grows and grows. Pacific Bell, for example, employs diversity managers, equal employment opportunity investigators, and affirmative ac-tion officers." "Why They Hate CCRI," *Weekly Standard* (October 28, 1996), p. 24.

16. See chapter 1, this volume.

17. As a survey of American business recently put it: "The American business scene has a clearly identifiable ethos. Where most other rich countries are devoted to conti-nuity, America is devoted to change—or, as some of its businessmen are increasingly fond of saying, to 'creative de-struction.' That makes it a unique laboratory, from which the whole world has something to learn." "Back on Top? A Survey of American Business," *Economist* (September 16, 1995), p. 4.

18. Even as late as 1899, there were only 207,514 busi-ness establishments across the entire United States, with an average number of twenty-three employees. See Charles Gide, *Principles of Political Economy*, trans. E. Row (Bos-ton: D.C. Heath and Company, 1924), pp. 171–72.

19. For the *locus classicus* on the separation of owner-ship and management in the corporation, leading to a "managerial capitalism," see Adolf A. Berle and Gardiner C. Means, *The Modern Corporation on Private Property* (New York: Harcourt, Brace & World, Inc., 1932).

20. Nobel laureate Coase summarized his view thus: "In my article on 'The Nature of the Firm' I argued that, although production could be carried out in a completely decentralized way by means of contracts between individuals, the fact that it costs something to enter into these transactions means that firms will emerge to organize what would otherwise be market transactions whenever their costs were less than the costs of carrying out the transactions through the market. The limit to the size of the firm is set where its costs of organizing a transaction become equal to the cost of carrying it out through the market. This determines what the firm buys, produces, and sells." R. H. Coase, *The Firm, the Market, and the Law* (Chicago: University of Chicago Press, 1988), p. 7. See also pp. 33–56, "The Nature of the Firm."

21. Posner succinctly summarizes his view in this way: "Contrast two methods of organizing production. In the first, the entrepreneur contracts with one person to supply the component parts, with another to assemble them, and with a third to sell the finished product. In the second, he hires them to perform these tasks as his employees under his direction. . . . The essence of the first method is that the entrepreneur negotiates with each of the three producers an agreement specifying the price, quantity, quality, delivery date, credit terms, and guarantees of the contractor's performance. The essence of the second method is that the entrepreneur pays the producers a wage—a price not for a specific performance but for the right to direct their performance. . . .

"In sum, the contract method of organizing economic activity encounters the problem of high transaction costs, the method of organizing economic activity through the firm, the problem of loss of control." Richard A. Posner, *The Economic Analysis of Law*, 4th ed. (Boston: Little Brown & Company, 1992), pp. 391–427, esp. 391–92.

22. The actions of some unions have, to some degree, thrown this process into reverse. It has become more efficient and less time-consuming for some corporations to shed certain operations, in favor of competitively priced suppliers.

23. On the "corporate raiders," Irwin Stelzer observes: "Many serious students of America's corporations, even those who were no fans of the so-called predators who mounted hostile takeovers in the 1980s, came to realize that something was not quite right with the way many large companies were being run. When Milken broke the commercial banks' monopoly of corporate credit by making it possible for non-establishment entrepreneurs (a.k.a. the 'predators') to raise money by selling high-yield bonds (disparagingly called 'junk' by the five percent of companies that until then were the only ones that could issue corporate debt, and by their generally 'white shoe' investment banking and law firms), he unleashed a new breed of entrepreneurs on over-manned and over-perked corporations. He also ameliorated what economists call the 'principal-agent problem.' That problem arises when the agent designated to act for a principal has incentives to behave in ways that are not in the interest of the principal he represents." "Are CEOs Overpaid?" *The Public Interest* (Winter 1997), p. 28.

24. Murray Weidenbaum, director of the Center for the Study of American Business, divides criticisms of corporate management into three categories: the board of directors is a "rubber stamp," consisting of an "old boy" network "that makes it personally unpleasant for directors to

question the performance of their peers"; the board is dominated by the CEO (CEOs serve as chairman of the board
in 80 percent of the larger corporations); and the board is
plagued with conflicts of interest. See "The Evolving Corporate Board," *CSAB Contemporary Issues Series*, no. 65
(May 1994), pp. 2–5.

25. Michael Useem observes the shifting pattern of corporate ownership: "In 1965, individual holdings constituted 84 percent of corporate stock, institutional holdings
16 percent. By 1990, the individual fraction had declined
to 54 percent, and the institutional fraction had risen to 46
percent. A closer look at the 1,000 publicly traded companies with highest market value during the latter 1980s and
1990s reveals much the same trend. Between 1985 and
1994 . . . the institutional share rose by more than a point
a year, topping the 50 percent threshold in 1990 and reach-
ing 57 percent by 1994." *Investor Capitalism: How Money
Managers Are Changing the Face of Corporate America*
(New York: Basic Books, 1996), p. 25.

26. Roberta Romano notes the growing proportion of
pension fund investment: "The percentage of corporate equity held by institutional investors generally, and by pension funds in particular, has increased exponentially over
the past few decades. From holding less than 1 percent in
1950, pension funds held 26 percent of corporate equity by
1989. Public pension funds are approximately 30 percent
of this sector." "The Politics of Public Pension Funds," *The
Public Interest* (Spring 1995), p. 44. Peter Drucker was one
of the first to notice this phenomenon in his *Unseen Revolution: How Pension Fund Socialism Came to America* (New
York: Harper & Row, 1976).

27. See Michael P. Smith, "Shareholder Activism by

Institutional Investors: Evidence from CalPERS," *Journal of Finance*, vol. 51, no. 1 (March 1996), pp. 227–52. As the socialist writer Richard Mimms points out: "By 1994 the world-wide accumulated assets of pension funds totalled $10,000 billion, equivalent to the market value of all the companies quoted on the world's three largest stock markets." "The Social Ownership of Capital," *New Left Review*, vol. 219 (September/October 1996), p. 43.

28. As the U.S. Department of Labor itself says in its *1995 Report on the American Work Force:* "Several types of statistics are available to indicate whether there have been shifting trends in job stability. These include data on job tenure, retention rates, job turnover, and part-year work. All suggest that there has been little change in overall job stability." Quoted in Karl Zinsmeister, "Indicators: Special Edition on Economic Anxiety," *The American Enterprise* (July/August 1996), p. 18. This July/August issue presents many revealing charts and figures. Among the most interesting are these two:

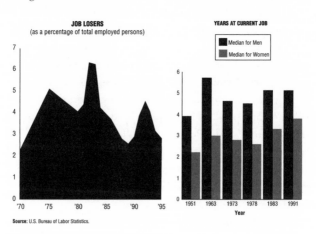

JOB LOSERS
(as a percentage of total employed persons)

YEARS AT CURRENT JOB

■ Median for Men
■ Median for Women

Source: U.S. Bureau of Labor Statistics.

29. Amity Shlaes stresses that most treatments complaining about AT&T's 40,000 layoffs leave out the fact "that communications and computer services, a sector that includes AT&T, created 408,000 new American jobs in the last four years, growing at a robust 4.6%." "A National Case of the Jitters," *Wall Street Journal*, June 4, 1996.

30. The conventional wisdom is that most new jobs are created by small businesses. The source most often quoted is the Small Business Administration, but in reporting job growth by small businesses, the SBA concentrates on small businesses that succeed, and ignores those that fail. Thus *net* job growth from small businesses is far smaller than often described. A brief account of how and why the conventional view is wrong—and how and why most job growth occurs in businesses employing 500 or more people—is found in David Hirschberg, "Small-Biz Blarney: What Does It Take to Kill a Bad Number," *Slate*, posted October 17, 1997.

31. As Al "Chainsaw" Dunlop says, "In my experience, the success of a company is inversely proportional to the size and opulence of the headquarters." Dunlop took over Scott Paper, a Fortune 500 conglomerate whose stock price was "in the basement" when it lost $277 million dollars in 1993. A bloated corporate staff was spending over $30 million a year on consultants and corporate perks. After two years of restructuring, sell-offs, and "shock therapy," Dunlop had virtually eliminated Scott's $2.5 billion debt and had increased the value of the company's shares from $2.5 billion in 1993 to $9 billion as of last year. Richard Miniter suggests that Dunlop did this by bringing "focus and energy to the executive suite" in "Al Dunlop and the Shareholder Revolution," *The American Enterprise* (November/December 1996), pp. 82–83.

32. According to Stelzer, "The chore of explaining and defending executive compensation is being made more difficult than need be by some corporate governance practices in need of reexamination. In many cases such compensation is set by board members who are themselves CEOs of other companies, who are often selected by the executives whose salaries they are to determine, and who are treated by those executives to a variety of 'perks,' ranging from use of the corporate jet to special pensions. When these board members convene to decide just how much to pay the company's chief executive officer, it is not seen by outsiders as a meeting of hard-nosed performance appraisers. And when they are assisted in their deliberations by compensation consultants who are also looking to the CEO for fee-rich assignments setting up company-wide benefits plans, the problem is compounded. And when corporate executives resist efforts by the regulators to have them reveal the estimated value of options they receive, and refuse to charge the present value of that sum against current earnings, suspicions that this may not be the most honest game in town understandably mount." "The Role and Governance of the Corporation," remarks delivered at the American Enterprise Institute's World Forum, June 22, 1996.

33. See "Business Should Act for All Its Stakeholders Before the Feds Do," *The CEO Series*, no. 9 (October 1996), pp. 5–7. I keep the author anonymous because, despite the glaring fault I am pointing out, his record as a corporate leader shows unusual courage and vigor in public argument. In this particular lecture, moreover, he deliberately selected an argument that (he judged) would persuade others in business, who are not as tuned in on the substance of the issues as he is. The fact that he felt an argument from

appeasement might be more likely of success, than simply laying out the challenge, sadly confirms the strength of the habit of appeasement.

34. Stuart Nolan, *Patterns of Corporate Philanthropy: Public Affairs Giving and the Forbes 250*, preface by Malcolm S. Forbes, Jr. (Washington, D.C.: Capital Research Center, 1994). This study should be taken as indicative, not probative, since corporate giving patterns are often closely held secrets. The actual records of some firms may be "better"—or "worse"—than the public materials available for this study suggest. Still, critics agree that while its reports on individual companies are unreliable because of the veil of secrecy, the study's general point is supported by a study of the actual funding received by antibusiness institutions. By law, these funding sources are made public in annual reports.

Appendix

1. An invention of mine, based on a fifteenth-century fable told by St. Bernardino of Siena, Italy. For more on St. Bernardino's economic thinking, see Alejandro A. Chafuen, *Christians for Freedom: Late Scholastic Economics* (San Francisco: Ignatius Press, 1986), and "What St. Bernardin's Ass Could Teach the Bishops," *Reason* (August/September, 1987), pp. 43–46.

Index

ABOUT THE AUTHOR

MICHAEL NOVAK holds the George Frederick Jewett Chair in Religion, Philosophy, and Public Policy at the American Enterprise Institute, where he is also director of social and political studies. In 1986, Mr. Novak headed the U.S. delegation to the Conference on Security and Cooperation in Europe. In 1981 and 1982, he led the U.S. delegation to the United Nations Human Rights Commission in Geneva. Mr. Novak has won the Templeton Prize for Progress in Religion, the Anthony Fisher Award, the Wilhelm Weber Prize, and the International Award of the Institution for World Capitalism, among others. The author of more than twenty-five books, he is also a cofounder and former publisher of *Crisis* and has been a columnist for both *National Review* and *Forbes*.